Ulrich Woitek

Business Cycles

An International Comparison
of Stylized Facts
in a Historical Perspective

With 45 Figures
and 45 Tables

Physica-Verlag

A Springer-Verlag Company

Series Editors
Werner A. Müller
Peter Schuster

Author
Dr. Ulrich Woitek
Seminar für Wirtschaftsgeschichte, SEMECON
Universität München
Ludwigstr. 33/IV
D-80539 München, Germany

ISBN 3-7908-0997-7 Physica-Verlag Heidelberg

Die Deutsche Bibliothek – CIP-Einheitsaufnahme
Woitek, Ulrich: Business cycles: an international comparison of stylized facts in a historical
perspective; with 45 tables / Ulrich Woitek. – Heidelberg: Physica-Verl., 1997
   (Contributions of economics)
   Zugl.: München, Univ., Diss., 1996
   ISBN 3-7908-0997-7

Softcover Design: Erich Kirchner, Heidelberg

SPIN 10566278   88/2202-5 4 3 2 1 0 – Printed on acid-free paper

To my parents

Preface

This study is a revised version of my doctoral dissertation at the Economics Department of the University of Munich (February 1996). I want to express my gratitude to Professor Claude Hillinger, the supervisor of this dissertation, for his help and encouragement during the last four years. I also thank Professor Gebhard Flaig for his critical comments.

Special thanks are due to my colleagues at SEMECON, especially Michael Reiter. I am indebted to Monika Sebold-Bender, Rudolf Köhne-Volland, and Markus Heintel for providing me with software, and to Robert Frank for reliable technical support.

Professor Hillinger made it possible for me to present a central part of this study at the *Conference on Dynamic Disequilibrium Modelling* in Munich. I want to thank the participants of this conference, especially Peter Zadrozny, for their helpful comments and suggestions.

Table of Contents

Chapter 1

Introduction

The study has two related purposes: First, I want to extend and deepen the empirical knowledge regarding the stylized facts of business cycles. Particular emphasis is placed upon the stability of empirical regularities by means of international and historical comparison. Moreover, a spectral analysis method relatively novel in the application to economic time series is presented and implemented. This method is Maximum Entropy (ME-) spectral analysis, which was developed during the 1960s and 1970s in the natural sciences. ME-spectral estimation is especially suitable for econometric purposes, since it efficiently extracts the information on the cyclical structure contained in very short time series. The application of the ME-spectrum to the analysis of business cycles was pioneered at SEMECON, University of Munich, but thus far only for univariate series. The present study extends this approach to the multivariate case.

Business Cycle Stylized Facts

In empirical business cycle research the regularity of economic fluctuations is an old finding, which goes back to the work of Clément Juglar. Based on the graphical analysis of financial series of France, United Kingdom, and the United States, Juglar (1889) identified a cycle of about ten years. Subsequent to Juglar, a sizeable literature on business cycles emerged. What is important in the present context is that by the 1940s and 1950s, certain features of the phenomenon were widely agreed upon. Hillinger (1992b), p. 26, gives an overview over this set of stylized facts: The inventory cycle (*Kitchin-cycle*),[1] with a duration of three to four years, the equipment cycle (*Juglar-cycle*), with a duration of seven to ten years, and the building cycle (*Kuznetz-cycle*),[2] with a length of about 20 years.[3] The length of each cycle was related to the speed with which the level of the associated capital stock could be adjusted.

In the 1960s, influenced by two decades of rapid and smooth economic growth, economists turned away from the study of business cycles. Connected with the vanishing interest in the phenomenon, the empirical knowledge embodied in the traditional view of business cycles also disappeared. During the 1970s, slowing and more erratic growth coupled with rising unemployment and inflation gave rise to a renewed interest in economic fluctuations. The new attempts at explaining fluctuations were monetarism, new classical economics and the real business cycle theory. The current view of business cycle stylized facts may be summarized as follows:

---

[1] The term *Kitchin-cycle* refers to Joseph Kitchin (1923), who discovered a short cycle with a length of 40 month (= 3.33 years) in time series of interest rates, commodity prices and clearings for the United States and the United Kingdom in the period 1890-1922.

[2] Kuznets (1958) found a cycle with a length of 22 years in economic variables. Other authors report similar results (15-25 years), see e.g. the overview in Abramovitz (1964).

[3] See e.g. the citation of Alvin Hansen (Samuelson (1961), p. 289-290):

> *The American experience indicates that the major business cycle has had an average duration of a little over eight years. Thus, from 1795 to 1937 there were seventeen cycles of an average duration of 8.35 years. [...]*
>
> *Since one to two minor peaks regularly occur between the major peaks, it is clear that the minor cycle is something less than half the duration of the major cycle. In the one hundred and thirty-year period 1807 to 1937 there were thirty-seven minor cycles with an average duration of 3.51 years. [...]*
>
> *[...] it appears that the building cycle averages somewhere between seventeen and eighteen years in length, or almost twice the length of the major business cycle. [...]*

The term "business cycle" is a misnomer insofar as no unique pe-
riodicities are involved, but its wide acceptance reflects the recog-
nition of important regularities of long standing. The observed
fluctuations vary greatly in amplitude and scope as well as du-
ration, yet they also have much in common. First, they are
national, indeed often international, in scope, showing up in a
multitude of processes, not just in total output, employment, and
unemployment. Second, they are persistent – lasting, as a rule
several years, that is, long enough to permit the development of
cumulative movements in the downward as well as upward direc-
tion. [...] For all their differences, business expansions and con-
tractions consists of patterns of recurrent, serially correlated and
cross-correlated movements in many economic (and even other)
activites.

(Zarnowitz (1992), p. 22)

Based on this definition, lists of stylized facts as the one in Lucas (1977),
p. 217, refer to comovements, not to cyclical structure:

(i) Output movements across broadly defined sectors move to-
gether. [...] (ii) Production of producer and consumer durables
exhibits much greater amplitude than does the production of non-
durables. (iii) Production of and prices of agricultural goods and
natural resources have lower than average conformity. (iv) Busi-
ness profits show high conformity and much greater amplitude
than other series. (v) Prices generally are procyclical. (vi) Short-
term interest rates are procyclical; long-term rates slightly so.
(vii) Monetary aggregates and velocity measures are procyclical.

This contemporary view of business cycles is seen to be considerably less
specific than the traditional one, especially in that it does not postulate
periodicities. It will be shown in this study that it is possible to get much
more detailed information on the structure of economic fluctuations by means
of ME spectral analysis. More concretely, our method is able to answer the
following questions:

1. Are the observed fluctuations irregular or do they show cyclical structure, i.e. do they exhibit on average maxima and minima at regular
   time intervals?

2. If they show cyclical structure, how many cycles can be identified?

3. What can be said about the length of these cycles?

4. How important are they, i.e. how large is the part of the variance of the fluctuations that can be explained by a particular cycle, how strong is the influence of the noise?

5. What can be said about the lead-lag relationships between cycles in different series?

Since we want to investigate the importance of cycles, it is natural to adopt the frequency domain approach, i.e. to use spectral analysis. For reasons discussed below, this is not the usual method for describing business cycle stylized facts, although it has a long tradition in macroeconometrics. In modern studies, time domain methods are prevailing. One of the aims of this study is to show that ignoring the frequency domain is not justified: Information on business cycle structure obtained by spectral analysis is more detailed than that obtained by time domain methods.

Stylized Facts and Explanatory Theories

The SEMECON research program on business cycles assigns a central role to the determination of stylized facts. This emphasis corresponds to the methodology of the natural sciences and stands in contrast to that of main stream econometrics. Natural scientists endeavour to establish empirical regularities, for example the elliptical orbits of the planets. Prediction in the natural sciences means prediction of such regularities, not of individual data points.

In the context of business cycles the relationship between empirical regularities or stylized facts and explanatory theories may be illustrated by two examples taken from earlier work at SEMECON. A stylized fact confirmed in the present study is that the short inventory cycle does only seldomly appear in the data on fixed investment, but that the long equipment cycle is prominent in the data on inventory investment in addition to the short cycle. This stylized fact was first observed after it was seen to be a prediction of a model of the interaction between the two cycles (Hillinger and Reiter (1992)). A second stylized fact which has been noticed by several observers is that business cycles often exhibit a typical M-shape which involves an alternation of mild and severe recessions. This phenomenon requires the long and the short cycle to be locked in a certain phase relationship. Precisely such a lock is predicted by Weser's theory of the aggregation of business cycles (Weser (1992)).

The methodology of main stream econometrics is derived from statistics, not from the basic natural sciences.[4] From a pragmatic point of view, it can simply be stated that the testing approach of econometrics has not led to the expected growth in validitated empirical knowledge an related explanatiory theories. As Summers (1991), p. 132 has put it:

> *Theoretical particle physicists wait anxiously to see whether exper-imentalists will be able to identify the particles their theories pos-tulate.[...] The image of an economic theorist nervously awaiting the result of a decisive econometric test does not ring true. The negligible impact of formal econometric work on the development of economic science is manifest in a number of ways.*

A certain revival of interest in business cycle stylized facts with the real business cycle theory. The reason is that the difficulty of econometric es-timation and testing of those models has driven their proponents to the alternative of calibration of the models in relation to stylized facts. In spite of the recent interest it cannot be said that a satisfactory methodology for establishing stylized facts has evolved in econometrics.[5] To demonstrate the superiority of the frequency domain approach over time domain methods in

---

[4] The problematic nature of statistical testing in econometrics and the natural science alternative are discussed in Hillinger (1992a) and Reiter (1995), pp. 9-12.

[5] Two recent German textbooks on business cycles (Maußner (1994) and Tichy (1994)), which consider the traditional as well as the modern approaches, are noteworthy for their emphasis on stylized facts in relation to explanatory theories.

the determination of business cycle stylized facts is a principal aim of this study.

The study is structured as follows: In Chapter 2, the method is illustrated using the German postwar data set as example. Chapter 3 contains a detailed description of ME spectral analysis. The principal empirical results are discussed in Chapter 4. An application is presented to the univariate and multivariate stylized facts of business cycle fluctuations for 11 OECD countries.[6] These stylized facts are compared with results from the literature and with findings for historical macroeconomic time series. Chapter 5 concludes with a summary of the outcome. The appendix contains a discussion of the long-run characteristics of the GDP-series under analysis.

---

[6] Australia, Canada, Denmark, France, Germany, Great Britain, Italy, Japan, Norway, Sweden, United States.

Part I

The Methodology

Chapter 2

Illustrating the Methodology: The Case of Germany

2.1 Introduction

To obtain a first insight regarding the cyclical structure of a time series $X_t, t = 1, \ldots, N$, usually the sample autocovariance function of the series is computed, given by

$$
\begin{aligned}
\hat{\gamma}_x(\tau) &= \frac{1}{N} \sum_{t=\tau+1}^{N} (X_t - \bar{X})(X_{t-\tau} - \bar{X}); \\
\tau &= 0, 1, \ldots, N-1
\end{aligned}
\tag{2.1}
$$

where $\bar{X}$ denotes the sample mean. This function measures the degree of the linear relationship between two observations in the same series. High values of the autocovariance function at lag τ indicate that the series exhibits cyclical structure with a cycle length of about τ units of time. The cross covariance function, given by

$$
\begin{aligned}
\hat{\gamma}_{xy}(\tau) &= \frac{1}{N} \sum_{t=\tau+1}^{N} (X_t - \bar{X})(Y_{t-\tau} - \bar{Y}); \\
\tau &= 0, 1, \ldots, N-1
\end{aligned}
\tag{2.2}
$$

measures the degree of the linear relationship between two observations in the series X and Y. Using the cross-covariance function we are able to analyze the lead-lag structure of the two series. If the two functions are normalized using the sample variances, we obtain the sample auto- and cross-correlations. Although the information obtained in this way is useful, it remains limited, as will be shown in the following.

A description of the typical procedure of describing business cycle stylized facts can be found in Kydland and Prescott (1990), p. 9.[1] They provide information on the following three aspects of business cycle characteristics:

- *The amplitude of fluctuations*
- *The degree of commovement with real GDP*
  (our measure of pro- or countercyclicality)
- *The phase shift of a variable relative to the overall business*
  cycle, as defined by the behaviour of cyclical real GNP.

They start their analysis with a comparison of the volatility of macroeconomic time series[2] using the standard deviation. Then, they examine the the GDP-fluctuations. These results are used as reference cycles with which the cyclical structure in the other series can be compared. The comovement with the GDP-cycle can be seen from the cross-correlation at lag 0. If the cross-correlation is close to 1, the series is highly *procyclical*; if the cross-correlation is close to -1, the series is *countercyclical*. If the cross correlation is close to 0, the series is uncorrelated with the reference cycle.

In addition, they use the cross-correlations to examine the lead-lag relationship between the GDP-cycle and the other series. If the cross-correlation reaches high values for a lag $\tau > 0$, the series *leads* the reference cycle, i.e. reaches its turning points τ units of time earlier than the GDP. In the other case, if the cross correlation is high for a lag $\tau < 1$, the series' cycle *lags* behind the GDP cycle by τ units of time.

---

[1] See also Backus and Kehoe (1992).

[2] US quarterly data, 1954-1989, deviations from the Hodrick-Prescott trend in per cent (see Appendix A).

In the following section, a comparison of this standard procedure with the methodology of the study at hand is given to show that spectral analysis methods are superior for the description of business cycle stylized facts. As an example, a data set of the German GDP and its components is used.[3] The components are: Gross Fixed Capital Formation (GFCF), Inventory Investment (II), Private Consumption (CP), Governmental Consumption (CG), Exports (EX), and Imports (IM). The analysis starts with a simple visual examination of the data. Then, the time domain methods described above are applied. In the next step, the spectra of the GDP and its components are estimated and the results are compared with the outcome for the time domain.

2.2   Visual Analysis

Visual examination of a time series is an important initial step in the analysis of data characteristics. Looking at the plot of the series, one obtains first information on the data, in our case on the cyclical structure. This first insight can be reinforced by simple data transformations such as taking growth rates, in order to bring out characteristic features, for example the importance of the fluctuations relative to the trend component, or the regularity of

---

[3] 1969-1989, annual data (data source: OECD Statistical Compendium, 1994). The series stops in 1989 in order to avoid problems with the structural break due to the turmoils of German reunification. Annual data are used throughout this study despite of the fact that in the main part of the literature on business cycle stylized facts quarterly data are analyzed. But a larger data base does not necessarily mean that the estimates become more reliable. Using quarterly data for our purpose would cause additional problems. If one decides to use seasonal adjusted data, one would have to take into account the distortions of the data structure caused by the usually applied adjustment procedures like the X11-method. Since from official statistics it is seldom possible to get the necessary information, it would not be clear whether the structure of the data under analysis is spurious or not.

If 'raw' data are used, one would have to decide first the exact nature of the seasonal component, i.e. to decide between stochastic and deterministic seasonality, which is a comparably difficult task as the decision between trend and difference stationarity described in Appendix A (For an overview on the problem of seasonality, see Hylleberg (1992)).

the fluctuations. The outcome can be used to decide the further procedure and to check the results of the more sophisticated methods for plausibility.

Figure 2.1 contains the plots of the data in logs.[4] The first impression one obtains from Figure 2.1 is that GDP, CP, CG, EX, and IM (Figure 2.1 (a), (d), (e), (f), and (g)) are dominated by the trend component, while the two investment series (GFCF and II, Figure 2.1 (b) and (c)) are much more volatile. Examining the GDP in more detail, we see that there are fluctuations around the trend, with troughs in the years 1967, 1975, and 1982. These troughs can also be detected in CP and IM, but they are not as obvious in CG and EX.

Apparently fixed investment and inventories are responsible for the GDP-fluctuations. The presence of a cycle is striking in GFCF, while the trend is not as important as in GDP. The major troughs are in the years 1967, 1975, and 1982. Inventories do not exhibit a trend component, but fluctuate rather irregularily. Deep troughs can be seen in the years 1967, 1975, and 1982. More moderate troughs can be found in 1967, 1971, 1978, and 1987. All in all the plot of II resembles the well-known '*M-shape of the business cycle*', as it is reported by e.g. Helmstädter (1989). This M-shape, which can be seen in the periods 1967-1975 and 1975-1982 appears to be due to a superposition of a long cycle with a length of about 7-8 years and a shorter cycle of about 3-4 years. The troughs of the short cycle lead to an amplification of the troughs of the long cycle, while the peaks of the long cycle are reduced.

---

[4] The exception is II, which is in DM at 1985 prices.

Fig. 2.1: The German GDP and its Components, 1960-1989

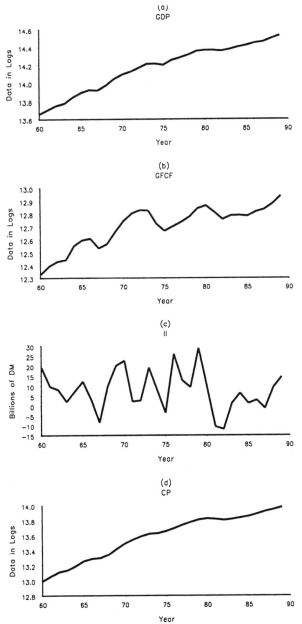

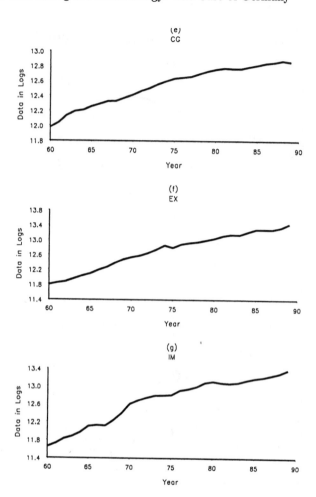

In Figure 2.2 the growth rates of the German GDP and its components are plotted. Taking growth rates has two effects on the structure of the series: The trend is to a large extent eliminated from the data. The relative amplitude of the shorter fluctuations and the influence of the irregular component is amplified.[5]

Again, II is an exception. This series does not have a growth component and is sometimes negative; therefore, growth rates cannot be computed. Instead, a first order difference filter is applied to the data, which has a similar effect on the data structure.

We see that for all series, the trend is to a large extend eliminated, with the exception of the growth rates of CP and CG (Figure 2.2 (d) and (e)), which exhibit a distinct downward trend. The GDP growth rates (Figure 2.2 (a)) now show the M-shape, i.e. the superimposed cycles with a length of 7-8 and 3-4 years. The major troughs are located in the years 1967, 1975, and 1982. Minor troughs can be seen in the years 1963, 1971, 1977/78, and 1987. The growth rates GFCF and CP (Figures 2.2 (b) and (d)) exhibit only the long cycle with troughs in the years 1967, 1974, and 1981/82. The long cycle can no longer be found in the first differences of II (Figure 2.2 (c)); the series is dominated by the short cycle and the irregular fluctuations. The growth rates of IM (Figure 2.2 (g)) have similar cyclical characteristics as the GDP growth rates. Actually, IM is not a component of aggregate demand, but contributes together with foreign production to satisfy this demand. Therefore, the obvious similarity of the fluctuations means that IM has a stabilizing effect on the business cycle. The fluctuation of the growth rates of CG and EX (Figure 2.2 (e) and (f)) is rather irregular.

---

[5] For details, see Appendix A.

Fig. 2.2: The German GDP and its Components, Growth Rates, 1961-1989

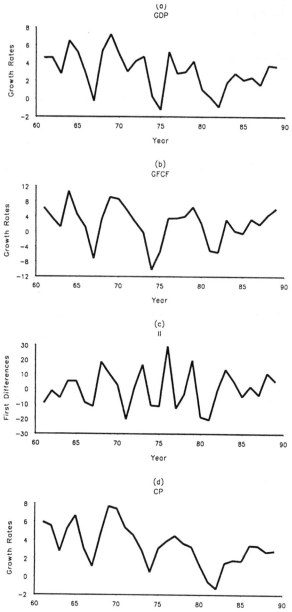

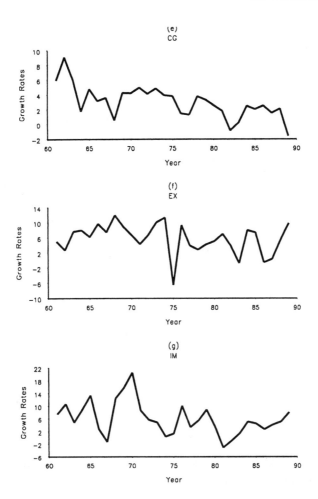

The detrended German GDP and its components are displayed in Figure 2.3. The Hodrick-Prescott filter (Hodrick and Prescott (1980)) is the method of choice of Kydland and Prescott (1990) and Backus and Kehoe (1992); since their papers are chosen as examples for the standard procedure, it is consistent to apply the same detrending method. However, it should be noted that given the problem of spurious cyclical structure, applying a detrending procedure without analyzing the type of non-stationarity cannot be recommended.[6]

A look at the plots in Figure 2.3 reveals that for the purpose of visual examination, the detrended data provide similar information as the above results. Since the data transformation differs, this similarity confirms that the cyclical structure found in the series is not artificial. The fluctuations are now much more regular than after taking growth rates, and the turning points match more closely.

The detrended GDP (Figure 2.3 (a)) is dominated by the long cycle. The major troughs are located in the years 1967, 1975, and 1982/83. The short cycle is not as distinct as in the growth rates; minor troughs are found in the years 1963, 1970, and 1987. The pattern of the detrended GFCF and CP (Figure 2.3 (b) and (d)) exhibit a very regular long cycle. The troughs are located in the years 1967/68, 1975, and 1981/84. Again, II (Figure 2.3 (c)) shows both the long and the short cycle, the short cycle being obviously more important than in the detrended GDP. The fluctuations of IM (Figure 2.3 (g)) seem to be not as regular as the fluctuations in GDP, but at least the troughs are located in the same years. In CG and EX (Figure 2.3 (d) and (f)), obvious cyclical structure cannot be detected by visual analysis.

---

[6] See Appendix A for a discussion.

Fig. 2.3: The German GDP and its Components, Detrended Series, 1960-1989

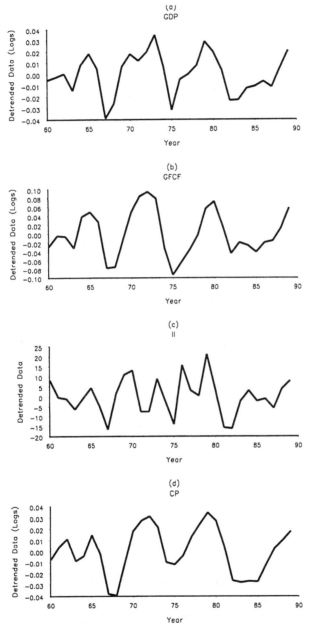

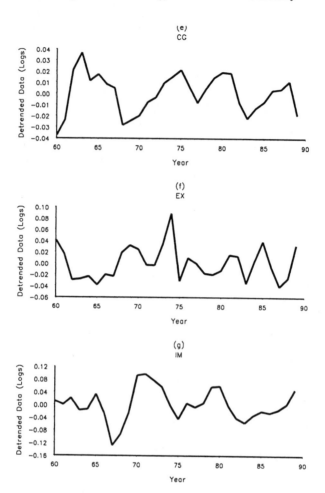

It is obvious that there is a kind of regularity in the data, which resembles the quasi-cycle as defined by Frisch (1933b). Summing up, we obtain the following result:

The German GDP is dominated by the trend component. Around this trend, one observes a rather regular fluctuation with a length of about 7-8 years. In addition, a superimposed short cycle with a length of 3-4 years can be detected in the growth rates. These cycles are mainly due to the fluctuations in the investment series. GFCF exhibits the long cycle, while the structure of the inventory fluctuations is dominated by the short cycle. The long cycle can also be found in CP and IM. The fluctuations of CG and EX are more irregular.

2.3   Time Domain Methods

In Table 2.1 additional information on the data characteristics of the German GDP and its components is given, following Reiter (1995), pp. 27-28.

Table 2.1: The German GDP and its Components: Descriptive Statistics

	(1)	(2)	(3)	(4)
GDP	100.00	2.09	100.00	-
GFCF	22.54	5.20	55.99	59.11
II	0.49	121.35	28.26	92.81
CP	56.47	2.32	62.66	52.45
CG	19.47	1.47	13.65	99.40
EX	26.95	5.27	67.76	80.21
IM	25.96	5.64	69.89	166.52

(1) mean of component / mean of GDP (per cent)

(2) standard deviation (sd) of detrended component / mean of component (per cent)

(3) sd of detrended component / sd of detrended GDP (per cent)

(4) sd of (detrended GDP - detrended component) / sd of detrended GDP (per cent)

In column (1) a measure for the share of a component in the of GDP (in levels) is displayed. It can be seen that CP contributes the largest part by far to total GDP with a share of 56 per cent. The share of the II-component is less than 1 per cent. GFCF, EX, and CG have an average share of about 20 per cent. From the sum of the share of these components, the 26 per cent for IM have to be substracted to add to 100 per cent.

In column (2) we have a measure for the variability of the series: the ratio of the standard deviation (sd) of the detrended series (Hodrick-Prescott filter) to the mean of the series. II fluctuates extremely with 120 per cent. CG and CP are least variable (2-3 per cent). Since they contribute together the largest part to GDP, they cause the aggregate to be relatively smooth (2 per cent). The variability of GFCF, EX, and IM is intermediate (5 per cent).

In Column (3) the ratio of the sd of a detrended component relative to the sd of GDP is displayed. The value for EX and IM is largest (about 70 per cent). Given that IM is a substitute for domestic production, this result means that they stabilize the business cycle. GFCF and CP contribute about 55-60 per cent to GDP-fluctuations. The value for II is 30 per cent; CG has the lowest value (about 15 per cent).

In column (4) the importance of a particular component for the variability of the detrended GDP is measured using the ratio of the sd of (detrended GDP minus[7] the detrended component) to the sd of the detrended GDP. The sd of the detrended GDP remains more or less unchanged if substracting CG, II, and EX. The destabilizing effect of CP is highest and for GFCF. Again it can be seen that the imports have a stabilizing effect on the fluctuations of GDP.

Summing up the results it can be seen that the investment series play an important role for the GDP-fluctuations, although they are not the largest components. But these measures provide only information on the overall variability of the GDP and its components, not on the regularities we have detected in the visual analysis. In order to analyze the cyclical structure of the series in the time domain, the autocorrelation of GDP and the cross correlations with the components are displayed in Table 2.2 on the following page.[8] To get a visual impression of the structure of these functions, they are plotted in Figures 2.4 and 2.5.[9] Figure 2.4 shows all of the autocorrelations which are not in the table.

---

[7] 'plus' in the case of IM.

[8] The table follows Kydland and Prescott (1990). Only the values for the autocorrelation of GDP are displayed to identify the reference cycle. The cross correlations with the components indicate whether the series is pro- or countercyclical and provide information on the lead-lag relationships (see p. 10).

[9] All data are again in logs (with the exception of II), i.e. the detrended data are percentage deviations from the trend. To compute the cross correlations between GDP and II, GDP is left in levels.

Table 2.2: The German GDP and its Components: Cross-Correlations

				Cross Correlation of GDP at Time t with					
	$t-4$	$t-3$	$t-2$	$t-1$	t	$t+1$	$t+2$	$t+3$	$t+4$
GDP	-0.28	-0.31	-0.19	0.45	1.00	0.45	-0.19	-0.31	-0.28
GFCF	-0.49	-0.37	-0.06	0.49	0.88	0.44	-0.20	-0.46	-0.45
II	0.02	-0.14	-0.50	-0.22	0.59	0.45	0.09	0.12	0.09
CP	-0.40	-0.36	-0.06	0.51	0.85	0.56	0.05	-0.23	-0.40
CG	-0.18	0.02	0.36	0.43	0.14	-0.09	-0.20	-0.19	-0.36
EX	0.27	0.10	-0.04	0.14	0.20	-0.18	-0.08	0.16	0.32
IM	-0.36	-0.37	-0.12	0.47	0.86	0.50	0.01	-0.21	-0.35

Fig. 2.4: The German GDP and its Components, Autocorrelation Function

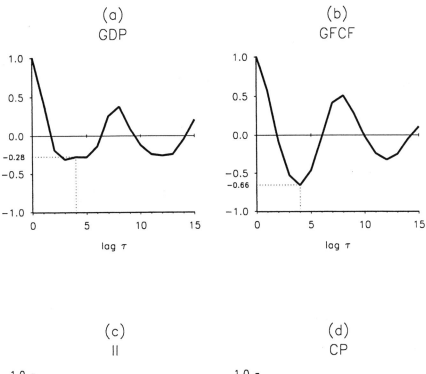

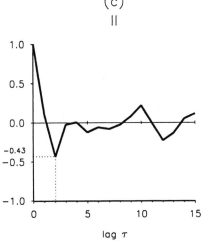

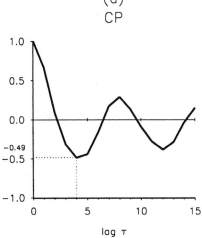

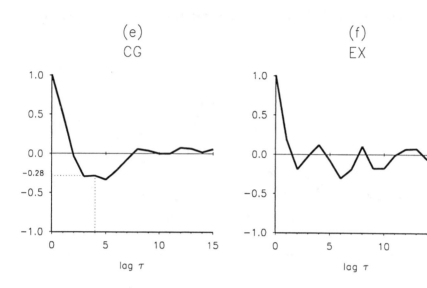

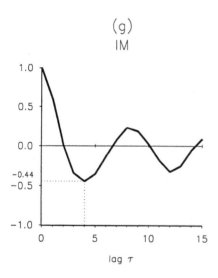

Fig. 2.5: The German GDP and its Components, Cross Correlations

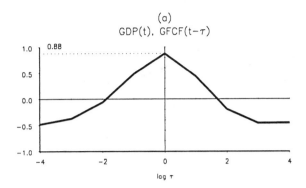

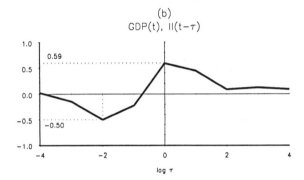

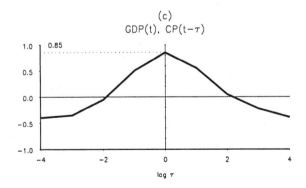

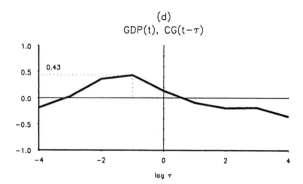

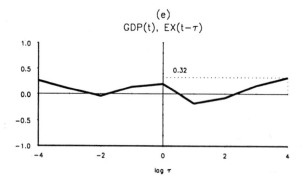

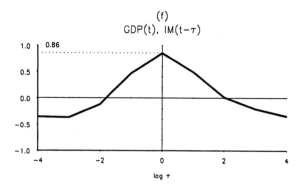

The sample autocorrelations of detrended GDP (Figure 2.4 (a); Table 2.2, first row) exhibit an obvious cyclical structure. At lag $\tau = 3$ and $\tau = 4$, they have values of about -0.3, i.e. the detrended GDP is negatively autocorrelated at these lags. This means that there is a cycle with a length of about 8 years in GDP, a result which was to be expected from the visual analysis above. The short cycle, which we detected in the GDP growth rates (see Figure 2.2 on p. 16), cannot be seen in the correlogram.

Comparing the results for the GDP-correlogram with the autocorrelations of the components we see that the long cycle is most distinct in the detrended GFCF (Figure 2.4 (b)). This component has the highest autocorrelation at lag $\tau = 4$ (-0.66). The correlograms of CP and IM (Figure 2.4 (d) and (g)) have a similar structure: At lag 4, the autocorrelation of detrended CP reaches a value 0f -0.49; for detrended IM, we have a value of -0.44.

Looking at the outcome for CG and EX, we see that there is no obvious cyclical structure to be detected. The autocorrelation of CG reaches a value of only -0.28 at lag 4. For EX, it might be possible to claim a cycle with a length of 4 years, but the respective peaks of the sample autocorrelations are very low.

The structure of the II correlogram is also rather irregular. But here, we have a relatively strong negative autocorrelation at lag $\tau = 2$ (-0.43), which indicates a short cycle with a length of 4 years in II. The long cycle, which we detected in the visual analysis of the original data (Figure 2.1 (c)) and the first differences (Figure 2.2 (c)), and which leads to the M-shape of the II-fluctuations, cannot be seen in the correlogram of the inventories.

Let us now turn to the cross correlations. Since we could only identify the 8 years long cycle in GDP, we have to use it as reference cycle and judge the correlation with the corresponding cycles in the components. Although obvious in the visual analysis, the short cycle has to be neglected. A first look at the plots in Figure 2.5 reveals that all components are procyclical, i.e. have positive cross correlations with the detrended GDP at lag 0. The correlation of GFCF (Figure 2.5 (a)) and CP (Figure 2.5 (c)) with GDP reaches very high values (0.88 and 0.85, see also Table 2.2 on p. 24). The value for the correlation between II and GDP at lag 0 is 0.59 (Figure 2.5 (b)); between the cycle in GDP and the cycles in CG and EX (Figure 2.5 (d) and (e)) the correlation is lowest (0.14 and 0.20).

If we use the term 'procyclical' as defined above and as it is used in the literature, IM is also procyclical to the GDP-cycle: The cross correlation peaks at lag $\tau = 0$ with a value of 0.86 (see Figure 2.5 (f) and Table 2.2, last row).[10] Since this component adds to GDP with a negative sign, the result from Table 2.1, column (4) is confirmed: Substracting the IM-cycle from the sum of the cycles in the other components leads to a reduction of the amplitude of the GDP-cycle.

What about the lead-lag relationships between the GDP-cycle and its components? We see that GFCF, CP and IM are strictly in phase, i.e. there is no peak in the cross correlations at lags $\tau \neq 0$. For II, we obtain negative cross correlations at lag $\tau = -2$ with a value of -0.5. This would mean that the GDP-cycle leads the II-cycle with a phase shift of 2 years. The peak at lag $\tau = 0$ indicates that the II-fluctuations are in phase. Taken together, this result reflect the correlation of the short II-cycle with itself.

Although not very strong (0.43), the correlation between detrended GDP and CG (Figure 2.5 (d)) show that the GDP-cycle leads the CG-cycle with a shift of 1 year. This result indicates that there is no anticyclical fiscal policy, but that CG passively follows the fluctuations of tax revenue caused by the general business cycle. From the plot of the correlations of detrended GDP and EX (Figure 2.5 (d)) no interpretable result can be derived, which is plausible since EX are determined by foreign demand. Hence, one would not expect a high correlation with the business cycle.

To sum up the results from the above section, the three aspects of business cycle characteristics cited on p. 10 are used as guideline:

---

[10] See also the results in Kydland and Prescott (1990), p. 14.

- Compared with the other GDP-components, the two investment series fluctuate extremely, especially II. According to Table 2.1, EX and IM fluctuate as much as GFCF.

- From the sample autocorrelations we find that the GDP-cycle has a length of about 8 years. Although present in the II-correlogram, the 4 years long cycle cannot be identified in the GDP.

- All GDP-components are procyclical. For IM this result means that it has a stabilizing effect. EX and CG show the weakest correlations with the GDP-cycle, GFCF, CP and IM the strongest.

As it was said in the introduction, this is useful information. But the analysis of the cyclical structure of German GDP and its components has shown the limitations of time domain methods: Regularities that can be detected by simple visual analysis cannot always be reproduced by the examination of the correlogram. We found this for the short cycle in GDP and the long cycle in II. It turns out to be extremely difficult to identify more than one cycle in the autocovariance function, and even if it were possible, one could hardly determine the relative importance of the cycles found in the series. In the following section a method will be presented which is able to solve these problems.

2.4   The Frequency Domain

A more powerful tool to describe the cyclical structure can be constructed by transforming the covariance function from the time domain into the frequency domain. This transformation is called *Fourier transformation*, and the result is the spectrum.

For the following, we need a first understanding of what a spectrum measures. A more detailed description of spectral analysis methods can be found in Section 3.2, but for the moment it is sufficient to concentrate on the classical spectral estimate, the *periodogram*, for which the interpretation is very easy to understand: Harmonic waves at a set of Fourier frequencies λ_j[11] are fitted to a series X_t using OLS. At this frequency set, the harmonic waves are uncorrelated. The resulting formula is given by

$$
\begin{aligned}
I_X(\lambda_j) &= A(\lambda_j)^2 + B(\lambda_j)^2; \\
A(\lambda_j) &= \sqrt{\frac{2}{N}} \sum_{t=1}^{N} X_t \cos 2\pi\lambda_j; \\
B(\lambda_j) &= \sqrt{\frac{2}{N}} \sum_{t=1}^{N} X_t \sin 2\pi\lambda_j;
\end{aligned}
\tag{2.3}
$$

To compare the fit of the cosines, their respective R^2s can be used. The plot of R^2 against the frequencies λ_j is called periodogram. Now assume that we find a (signifcant) peak at a frequency $\lambda^* = 0.125$ with an R^2 of 0.7. This would mean that the variance of a harmonic wave with a cycle length of about 8 years explains 70 per cent of the series' variance.

It can be shown that the resulting spectral estimate from equation (2.3) is, except for a constant term, equivalent to the Fourier transformation of the sample autocovariance function (see equation (2.1) on p. 9):

$$
I_x(\lambda_j) = \frac{1}{2\pi} \sum_{\tau=-N}^{N} \hat{\gamma}_x(\tau) e^{-i2\pi\lambda_j\tau};
\tag{2.4}
$$

In this way it is possible to describe the univariate cyclical structure, i.e. the relative importance of a cycle in the series under analysis. Computing the Fourier transform of the sample cross covariances of two series X and Y (see equation (2.2) on p. 9) gives an estimate for the cross-spectrum:

$$
I_{xy}(\lambda_j) = \frac{1}{2\pi} \sum_{\tau=-N}^{N} \hat{\gamma}_{xy}(\tau) e^{-i2\pi\lambda_j\tau};
\tag{2.5}
$$

Together with the univariate spectral estimates $I_x(\lambda_j)$ and $I_y(\lambda_j)$, $I_{xy}(\lambda_j)$

---

[11] $\lambda_j = j/N; j = 1, 2, \ldots, K$, where N is the number of observations, and K is $N/2$ if N is even and $(N-1)/2$ if N is odd (see e.g. Priestley (1981), p. 392).

can be used to compute multivariate spectral measures with which it is possible to examine the lead-lag relationship between cycles at the same frequency in different series.[12]

The term '*spectrum*' was introduced by Newton (1671), who used it to describe the band of light colors resulting from light passing through a glass prism, each color presenting a particular wavelength of light.[13] The mathematical foundations of spectral analysis go back to D. Bernoulli, L. Euler, and J. B. J. Fourier. In the midth of the 19th century, spectral analysis techniques were applied to examine the periodicity of phenomena like sunspots, tides etc. The phenomena analyzed in these first applications exhibit obvious cyclical structure, which made it possible to describe them using the techniques available at that time. The analysis of series with hidden periodicities became feasible when Sir Arthur Schuster (1898) introduced the '*periodogram*' as an estimate for the spectrum of a time series. Beginning with Moore (1914), economists adopted this technique to examine the cyclical structure of economic time series, which was a widely accepted empirical finding at that time.[14]

"*Empirical studies in econometrics appear to go through phases where different techniques become particularly popular*" (Granger and Engle (1983), p. 94). This statement seems to be especially true for the application of spectral methods in econometrics. Since the beginning of this century, the interest in spectral analysis is subjected to fluctuations, both concerning the application and the development of appropriate techniques.[15] These fluctuations seem to correspond to fluctuations in the interest in business cycles itself, as it is described by Zarnowitz (1985), p.524: "*Interest in business cycles is subject to a wave-like movement, waxing during and after periods of turbulence and depression, waning in periods of substantial stability and*

---

[12] See Section 3.2.

[13] This paragraph follows the description in Marple (1987), pp. 3-12.

[14] See e.g. Niehans (1992), pp. 545-547.

[15] "*Theoretical developments of time series methods have followed a rather cyclical pattern first emphasizing one domain, then the other*" (Koopmans (1983), p. 169).

continuing growth."

Empirical business cycle research was a dominant topic in applied econometric work until about 1950.[16] This can be seen from a passage in the editorial of the first volume of Econometrica by Frisch (1933a), p. 4, where besides general economic theory, statistical technique and statistical information, business cycle theory is counted among the four fields of special interest for econometricians.

An overview of applications of spectral analysis in this early period can be found in Cargill (1974). He lists the work of Henry L. Moore (1914), (1923), William H. Beveridge (1921), William L. Crum (1923), Edwin B. Wilson (1934), Benjamin Greenstein (1935), and Harold T. Davis (1941). These early contributions, which analyse data sets of about 100-400 observations, are rather impressive given that today's technical possibilities for the computation of the spectral estimates were not available.[17]

The application of the periodogram to the description of the cyclical structure of economic time series is not to be recommended. This problem will be discussed later on, but inspite of this, the univariate periodogram $I_X(\lambda_j)$ is sufficient as example to show the superiority of spectral methods for the description of business cycle stylized facts. In Figure 2.6 and Table 2.3, the univariate periodograms for the detrended[18] German GDP and its components are displayed. The multivariate analysis is left for the final part of the section, where a more appropriate spectral estimate is presented.

---

[16] See Morgan (1990), p. 11.

[17] The situation was even worse for natural sciences, although in some applications, mechanical harmonic analyzers could be used (see Marple (1987), pp. 4-5). Koopmans (1983), p. 169-170 writes:

> *The edge was taken off of the original enthusiasm for spectral domain techniques by the horrendous computational effort required to calculate numerical spectra. At that time, calculations had to be done by hand, and, although a number of simplified methods were developed, it was still a major undertaking to analyze time series of the magnitudes usually encountered in the physical sciences.*

[18] Hodrick-Prescott filter, see Appendix A.

Fig. 2.6: The German GDP and its Components, Periodograms

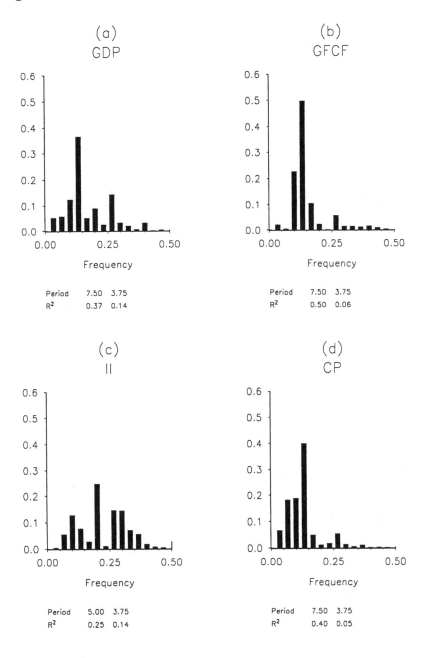

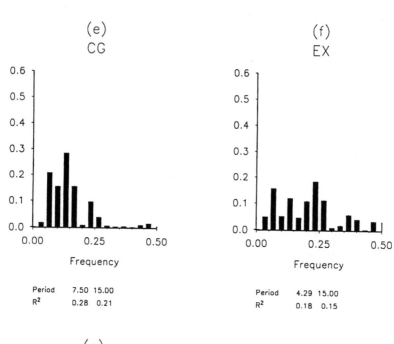

(e)
CG

Frequency

| Period | 7.50 15.00 |
| R^2 | 0.28 0.21 |

(f)
EX

Frequency

| Period | 4.29 15.00 |
| R^2 | 0.18 0.15 |

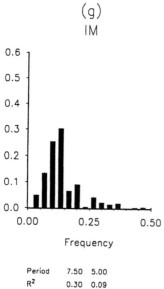

(g)
IM

Frequency

| Period | 7.50 5.00 |
| R^2 | 0.30 0.09 |

Table 2.3: The German GDP and its Components, Periodograms

GDP	Cycle Length	7.50	3.75
	R^2	0.37	0.14
GFCF	Cycle Length	7.50	3.75
	R^2	0.50	0.06
II	Cycle Length	5.00	3.75
	R^2	0.25	0.14
CP	Cycle Length	7.50	3.75
	R^2	0.40	0.05
CG	Cycle Length	7.50	15.00
	R^2	0.28	0.21
EX	Cycle Length	4.29	7.50
	R^2	0.18	0.12
IM	Cycle Length	7.50	3.75
	R^2	0.30	0.09

It is now possible to identify the short cycle detected in the visual analysis of the GDP above and to judge the relative importance of the two cycles. The GDP-periodogram (Figure 2.6 (a)) exhibits two peaks at cycle lengths of about 8 and 4 years. The long cycle is more important for the cyclical structure of the GDP. It has an R^2 of about 40 per cent. The R^2 for the short GDP-cycle is about 15 per cent.

From the periodograms of the component series we see that the long cycle is most prominent in GFCF (Figure 2.6 (b)), where it has an R^2 of 50 per cent. The cyclical structure of II (Figure 2.6 (c)) is dominated by short cycles with a length of 4-5 years. The 8 years long cycle we found above is not to be detected in the periodogram, at least not with sufficiently high R^2.

For the other components it can be said that the long cycle plays a similarly important role for CP (Figure 2.6 (d)) and IM (Figure 2.6 (g)), where it reaches R^2s of 40 and 30 per cent. The structure of CG and EX is least regular. In the periodogram of CG (Figure 2.6 (e)), a very long cycle with a length of 15 years can be found. With an observation period of about 30 years, this cycle length is clearly to long to be interpreted as a business cycle. As it was suspected in the analysis of the sample autocorrelations above, the fluctuations of EX are dominated by the short cycle with an R^2 of about 20 per cent, while the long cycle has an R^2 of only 10 per cent.

Given that the regularity in the fluctuations of economic time series can already be detected by simple visual examination of the plots, the periodogram seems to be the best method of choice to describe business cycle stylized facts. Compared with the time domain methods, univariate periodogram analysis provides much more detailed information on the cyclical structure of a time series. But as explained in the technical part below, the periodogram is not suited for the type of data one has to do with in macroeconometrics. This is one of the reasons why time domain methods are prevailing in the description of business cycle characteristics. Fortunately, there is another spectral estimate available: The *Maximum Entropy* (ME-) spectrum. This estimate was developed in the 60s and 70s in the natural sciences. The ME-spectrum, which turns out to be the spectrum of an autoregressive (AR-) process, has in general two advantages compared with the periodogram: It is based on more reasonable assumptions and is better suited for short time series.

Fitting AR-models to the data to analyze macroeconomic fluctuations is a widely accepted technique connected with the contributions of C. Sims (1980).[19] ME-spectral analysis just requires a further step: Computing the spectrum of the model estimated in the time domain. It was already fruitfully applied to the description of business cycle stylized facts.[20]

As was said above, the ME-spectrum can be looked upon as the spectrum of an AR-process. Therefore, if we want to analyze the univariate cyclical structure of the data, we first have to fit an AR-model of order p (AR(p)-model) to our series (see equation 3.15 on p. 68). If the multivariate cyclical structure is to be examined, a VAR-model (see equation 3.18 on p. 69) has

---

[19] For a discussion of Sims' methodology, see Darnell and Evans (1990). pp. 113 ff.

[20] See Hillinger and Sebold-Bender (1992), Reiter (1995), and Woitek (1996). A more detailed description can be found in Chapter 3.2 on p. 60.

to be fitted to the data set under analysis.[21]

Let us first take a look at the univariate cyclical structure. Each cyclical component in the model corresponds to a pair of complex conjugate roots of the characteristic polynomial (see equation 3.16 on p. 68), from which the cycle length and the modulus can be computed. Doing this for the detrended German GDP and its components, we obtain the results displayed in Table 2.4.

The modulus measures the extent to which a cycle is dampened. For example, a modulus of 0.91 as in the case of the long cycle in German GFCF, means that after one unit of time, the amplitude of the cycle is about 10 per cent smaller. The higher the modulus, the less the respective cycle is dampened.

For the German GDP, both the long and the short cycle can be computed from the roots of the characteristic polynomial. The long cycle is not as strongly dampened as the short cycle. Looking at the component series, we see that both cycles are present in the investment series. The long cycle has a higher modulus in GFCF, while the short cycle is more distinct in II. The cyclical structure of the other components is dominated by the long cycle, with the exception of EX. In this series, a cycle with a length of about 5 years can be detected, which has by far the smallest modulus (0.5).

---

[21] For the estimation procedure see Section 3.4.

Table 2.4: The German GDP and its Components, AR-Roots

	Complex Roots	Period	Modulus
GDP	$0.54 \pm i0.58$	7.70	0.79
	$0.18 \pm i0.64$	3.40	0.67
GFCF	$0.64 \pm i0.66$	7.82	0.91
	$0.24 \pm i0.62$	3.25	0.67
II	$0.27 \pm i0.69$	3.22	0.74
	$0.40 \pm i0.57$	6.51	0.67
CP	$0.56 \pm i0.59$	7.79	0.81
CG	$0.55 \pm i0.61$	7.51	0.83
EX	$0.13 \pm i0.49$	4.80	0.51
IM	$0.47 \pm i0.57$	7.12	0.74

The AR-models exhibit the same cyclical characteristics we found for the German GDP and its components by means of the periodogram. The next step in our analysis is to compute the univariate and multivariate spectra from our estimated models using the formulas explained in Section 3.2 on page 69 ff. (equations (3.17) and (3.19)). From these spectra, the following measures are computed:[22]

Univariate Measures

- Peak Power (pp)

  Suppose that the spectrum of a series exhibits a peak at a frequency of λ^*. Then, pp measures the part of the series variance that can be explained by the variance of harmonic waves with frequencies in the interval $[0.9\lambda^*, 1.1\lambda^*]$. pp is a measure for the relative importance of the cyclical components in a series, comparable to R^2 in periodogram analysis (see Figure 3.1 on p. 64, equation (3.7), p. 63).

- Bandwidth (bw)/Modulus

  bw measures the range (in years) in which a peak in the spectrum

---

[22] A detailed explanation of the spectral measures used in this study can be found in Section 3.2 on p. 60.

is reduced by one half. The broader the peak, the less distinct the respective cycle is, respectively, the more the cycle is dampened (see Figure 3.2 on p. 65). If two peaks in the spectrum are too close or a cycle is too strongly dampened, *bw* cannot be computed. In these cases equivalent information can be drawn from the modulus of the corresponding root in the characteristic polynomial.

- Signal-to-Noise Ratio (*SNR*)
  SNR measures the influence of the noise on a series. The smaller *SNR*, the more noise driven is the series (equation (3.8), 65).

Multivariate Measures

- Squared Coherency (*sc*)
  Suppose the spectra of two series X and Y exhibit peaks at a frequency λ^*. *sc* measures the extend of the linear relationship between the cycles in the two series (equation (3.10), p. 66). It can be interpreted in the same way as the correlation coefficient in a linear regression model. We will examine *sc* for the relationship between the cyclical structure in GDP and the respective component cycles.

- Phase Shift
  The phase shift measures the lead-lag relationship between two cycles of the same frequency in the series X and Y, i.e. the distance between the turnings of cycles with the same frequency (equation (3.13), p. 67). In the following, the phase lead of the GDP-cycle over the respective component cycle will be computed.

- Gain
  The gain measures the multiplicative change of the amplitude of a cycle in series Y if transformed to the series X (equation (3.14), p. 67). It is a measure for the difference between the amplitudes of cycles with the same frequency. In our case, we examine the change in the amplitude of the component cycle if transformed to the GDP-cycle.

For reasons explained in Section 3.2, the univariate measures are not computed from the diagonal elements of the spectral density matrix in equation (3.19), p. 69, although in principle, this would be possible. Instead, they are computed from the univariate AR-spectrum (equation (3.17), p. 69). The results for the detrended[23] series are displayed in Table 2.5 and in Figure 2.7. In addition to the AR-spectra, the *integrated spectra* are plotted in Figure 2.7. Following the explanation in Chapter 3 on page 63, they are used to compute *pp*; moreover, it is possible to judge the 'importance' of a cycle from the integrated spectrum: The steeper the ascent at a peak frequency, the more distinct is the respective peak in the spectrum.

Although we know from the roots of the characteristic polynomial of the AR-model for GDP that there is a short cycle present, it does not have a corresponding peak in the spectrum, but only a small hump on the right side of the peak of the long cycle (Figure 2.7 (a)). This is due to the fact that the short cycle in GDP is strongly dampened (modulus: 0.67, see Table 2.4 on p. 40). The long cycle in GDP has a length of about 8 years, with a *pp* of 0.2. The *SNR* has a value of 8.

Looking at the component spectra, again the earlier results are confirmed. The long cycle is most distinct in GFCF (Figure 2.7 (b)), where it has a *pp* of about 0.4, while the short cycle dominates the structure of II with a *pp* of 0.2 (Figure 2.7 (c)). In the other component series, the long cycle with a length of 7-8 years is prevailing with *pp*s of about 0.2-0.25, again with the exception of the EX-spectrum (Figure 2.7 (f)), which exhibits a peak at a cycle length of about 5 years.

Comparing the *SNR*s of the components with the *SNR* of GDP, we find that II and EX are more noise driven than GDP, while GFCF, CP, CG, and IM have a more regular structure. The highest *SNR*s can be found for CP and GFCF (*SNR*=13-14), while EX is the series with the lowest *SNR* (*SNR*=5).

Summing up, we see a long cycle of about 7-8 years length and a short

---

[23] Hodrick-Prescott filter, see Appendix A.

cycle with a length of 3-5 years in the spectra of the German GDP and its components. The short cycle in GDP is too strongly dampened to exhibit a distinct peak. These cycles are most prominent in the spectra of the investment series. The cyclical structure of fixed investment is dominated by the long cycle, while the short cycle is most important in the inventories. In the other series, the long cycle is dominating. II and EX are strongly noise driven, while the fluctuations of GFCF and CP are relatively regular.

Fig. 2.7: The German GDP and its Components, AR-Spectra

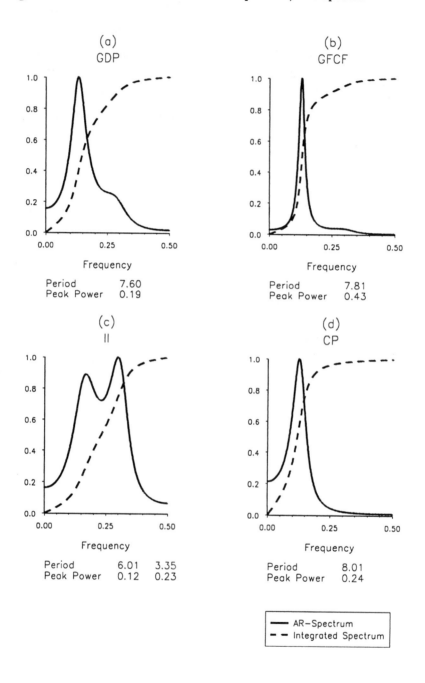

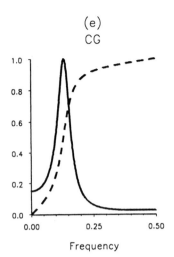

(e)
CG

Frequency

Period   7.61
Peak Power   0.26

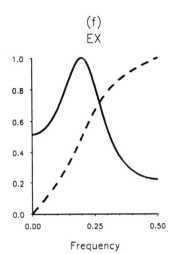

(f)
EX

Frequency

Period   5.05
Peak Power   0.14

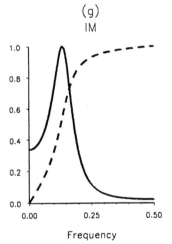

(g)
IM

Frequency

Period   7.45
Peak Power   0.19

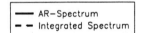

—— AR—Spectrum
– – Integrated Spectrum

Table 2.5: The German GDP and its Components, AR-Spectra

	Period	pp	bw	Moduli	SNR	AR-order
GDP	7.60	0.19	5.09	0.79	7.83	4
GFCF	7.81	0.43	1.82	0.91	13.55	4
II	6.01	0.12	-	0.70	5.85	4
	3.35	0.23	-	0.74		
CP	8.01	0.24	5.33	0.811	15.06	2
CG	7.61	0.26	4.06	0.83	9.82	3
EX	5.05	0.14	-	0.51	4.52	2
IM	7.45	0.19	8.72	0.74	10.05	2

In the next step, we compute the bivariate VAR-spectra of the detrended GDP and its components to judge the lead-lag relationship between the cyclical structure of the series. The results are displayed in Figures 2.8, 2.9, 2.10, 2.11, 2.12, and 2.13. The results in Table 2.6 must be interpreted in the following way:

We have three sensible possibilities to choose for which frequencies sc, gain, and phase are to be computed. First, we can compute the measures at the peak freuqencies of the GDP-autospectrum. This would be similar to the procedure found in the literature, where the cycle in aggregate output is used as reference cycle. Another possibility is to compute the measure at the peak frequencies of the respective component's autospectrum, which would have the advantage that the lead-lag relationship between a component cycle and the respective GDP-cycle can be analyzed, even if the GDP-cycle is too strongly dampened to exhibit a peak in the spectrum. The third possibility is to compute the measures for the peak frequencies in the coherence spectrum, in order to analyze the multivariate cyclical structure for frequencies where the coherence between the GDP-cycle and the component cycle is strongest.

In Table 2.6, the results for all three possibilities are presented. In Figures 2.8 - 2.13 only the outcome for the peaks of sc is displayed. It should be noted that for each of the 6 systems, the results in Table 2.6 are remarkably similar for all three possibilities.

Fig. 2.8: GDP/GFCF-Spectrum

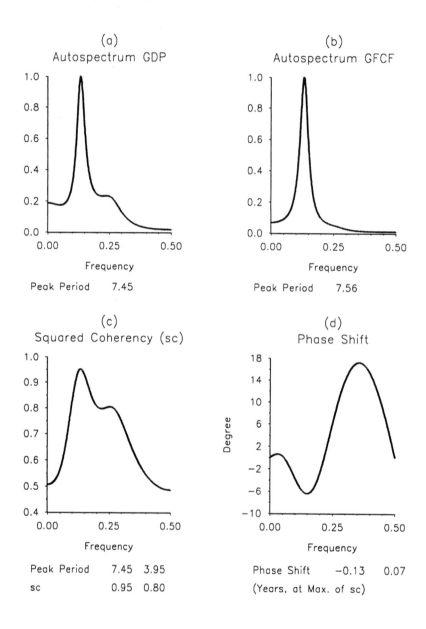

Fig. 2.9: GDP/II-Spectrum

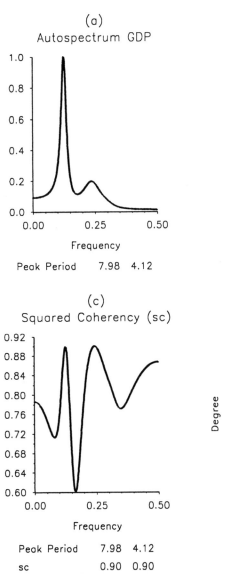

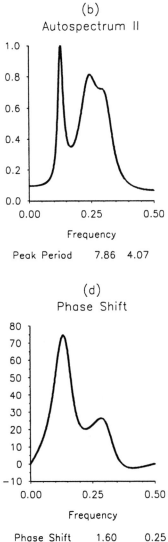

Fig. 2.10: GDP/CP-Spectrum

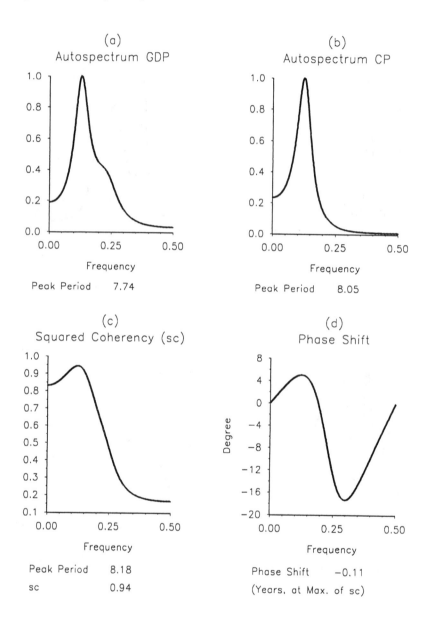

Fig. 2.11: GDP/CG-Spectrum

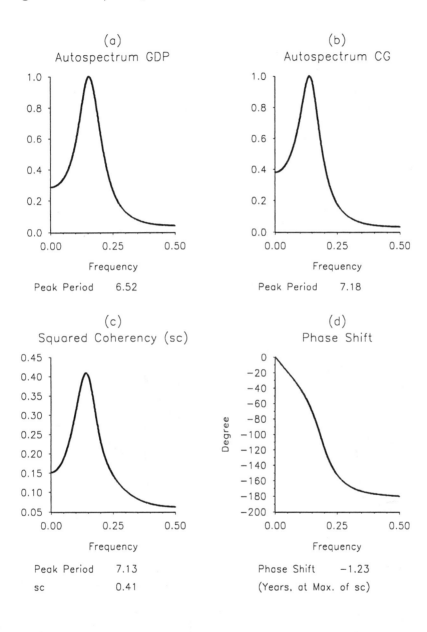

Fig. 2.12: GDP/EX-Spectrum

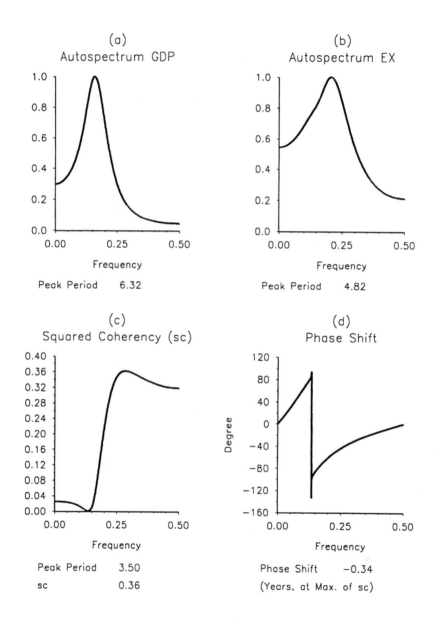

Fig. 2.13: GDP/IM-Spectrum

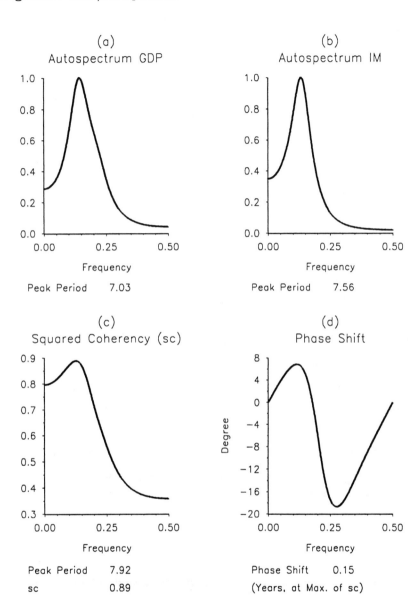

Table 2.6: The German GDP and its Components, Multivariate Spectra

		Period	sc	Phase	Gain	VAR-Order
GDP/GFCF	Max. of sc	7.45	0.95	-0.13	0.28	3
		3.95	0.80	0.07	0.56	
	Spectrum GDP	7.45	0.95	-0.13	0.28	
		4.19	0.80	0.04	0.52	
	Spectrum GFCF	7.56	0.95	-0.13	0.28	
GDP/II	Max. of sc	7.98	0.90	1.60	4.45	4
		4.12	0.90	0.25	2.16	
	Spectrum GDP	7.98	0.90	1.60	4.50	
		4.23	0.90	0.24	2.20	
	Spectrum II	7.86	0.90	1.60	4.40	
		4.07	0.90	0.25	2.14	
GDP/CP	Max. of sc	8.18	0.94	0.11	0.70	2
	Spectrum GDP	7.74	0.94	0.11	0.72	
	Spectrum CP	8.05	0.94	0.11	0.70	
GDP/CG	Max. of sc	7.13	0.41	-1.24	0.62	2
	Spectrum GDP	6.52	0.40	-1.31	0.64	
	Spectrum CG	7.18	0.41	-1.23	0.61	
GDP/EX	Max. of sc	3.50	0.36	-0.34	0.24	2
	Spectrum GDP	6.32	0.03	-1.44	0.13	
	Spectrum EX	4.82	0.24	-0.79	0.29	
GDP/IM	Max. of sc	7.92	0.89	0.15	0.29	2
	Spectrum GDP	7.03	0.88	0.12	0.31	
	Spectrum IM	7.56	0.89	0.14	0.30	

sc   : Squared Coherency

As it was to be expected, the autospectra have a slightly different shape than the univariate spectra. But in general, the cycle lengths for which the autospectrum reaches a maximum are about the same as in the univariate case. The GDP-autospectra have peaks at longer periods than the respective univariate spectrum. In the GDP/GFCF- and the GDP/II-system, the short cycle which did not exhibit a peak in the univariate GDP-spectrum (see Figure 2.7 (a) on p. 44) is now visible. Again with the exception of the GDP/EX-system, the cyclical structure of the other systems is dominated by a cycle with a length of 7-8 years.

The highest sc is reached by the GDP/GFCF-system at a cycle length of 7.45 years (0.95). The sc at the short cycle with a length of about 4 years is clearly smaller (0.8). Between GDP and II, the situation is reverse: Here, the short cycle has a slightly higher sc than the long cycle. As it was said above, the GDP/CP- and the GDP/IM-system are dominated by the long cycle. At these cycle lengths, the sc reaches values of about 0.9-0.95, although they are slightly smaller than for the long cycle in GDP and GFCF. The scs are smallest for the GDP/CG- and the GDP/EX-systems; for these series, the maximum values of sc are about 0.4.

The results for the lead-lag relationship between the GDP-cycles and the respective component cycles confirm and extend the outcome from the analysis in the time domain. The phase shift between the long cycle in GDP and the long cycle in GFCF is shorter than a year, i.e. the long cycle in GFCF is procyclical. The same result can be obtained for the short cycle in II and for the long cycles in CP and IM. The long GDP-cycle leads over the respective II-cycle with a phase shift of about one year. Now, we have a possible explanation for the shape of the cross-correlation between GDP and II (see Figure 2.5 (b) on p. 27): The short II-cycle is in phase, while the long II-cycle lags the long GDP-cycle.

The GDP-cycle lags the cycle in CG with a phase shift of about 1 year; this outcome is not consistent with the result from the time domain (see Figure 2.5 (d) on p. 27). But it should not be taken too serious, since the sc is very small. The phase shift between the cycles in GDP and in EX has the sign one would expect from the results of the correlation analysis, but again, sc is very small compared with the other systems. Therefore, this outcome has to be interpreted with caution.

As mentioned above, the gain spectrum measures the multiplicative change of the amplitude of a cycle in the component series if transformed to the GDP-series. Mind that with the exception of the GDP/II-system, all data are in logs. Hence, we analyze the cyclical structure of percentage deviations from the trend.

The amplitude of the cycles in GDP are smaller than the amplitudes of the investment cycles. The long GDP-cycle has an amplitude which is about 70 per cent smaller than the amplitude of the long cycle in GFCF. The same result is obtained for the long cycle in IM. The amplitude of the long cycle in CP and CG is only slightly smaller than the amplitude of the respective GDP-cycle. Again, the results for EX and CG are difficult to be interpreted because of the small *scs*. Since the data for the GDP/II-system are in levels, not in logs, the gain has another interpretation. For II, we see that the amplitude of the long cycle is about 4 times smaller than the amplitude of the GDP-cycle. The amplitude of the short cycle has to be multiplied by 2 to obtain the amplitude of the short GDP-cycle.

Summing up, we have the following results for the German business cycle:

1. In the GDP, a long cycle can be found with a length of about 7-8 years. This long cycle can also be seen in GFCF, CP, CG, and IM. The cyclical structure of EX and II is dominated by a short cycle with a length of about 4-5 years.

2. Between the cyclical structure in GFCF and in the GDP, there is a very strong coherence. Similar results are obtained for CP and IM. For EX and CG, the coherence is smallest. For the short cycle, the coherence is strongest between GDP and II.

3. The cycles in the investment series are procyclical, with the exception of the long II-cycle: This cycle lags behind the GDP-cycle with a phase shift of about 1 year.

4. In general, the GDP-cycle (percentage deviations from the trend) has smaller amplitudes than the respective cycles in the component series.

The results suggest that the cyclical structure in GDP is mainly due to the investment series. Inertia of investment caused by adjustment costs leads to investment overshooting and thus to the observed cyclical behaviour of fixed investment. The amplitude of the GDP-cycles (percentage deviations from the trend) is in general smaller than the amplitude of the respective component cycles, because production cannot be adjusted at once to unexpected demand fluctuations. To some extend, these fluctuations are neutralized by changes in inventories. Moreover, the imports have a smoothing effect on the business cycle by subsituting domestic production.[24]

In Chapter 4, the analysis is extended to the cyclical structure of price level and money stock data. Moreover, the question whether the results for the German example can be looked upon as typical will be answered by comparing them with the outcome for a number of OECD-countries. In the following chapter, spectral analysis methods and their application in econometrics are discussed in more detail.

---

[24] This explanation is part of the *Second-Order Accelerator* models of cyclical behavior developed by C. Hillinger (see Hillinger, Reiter and Weser (1992a), Hillinger and Reiter (1992), and Reiter (1995)).

Chapter 3

Spectral Analysis

3.1 Introduction

Beginning with the work of Moore (1914) and (1923), the application of spectral estimation to economic time series is subjected to changes in popularity. Since the publication of the influential book by Box and Jenkins (1970), the time-domain approach is prevailing in the description of business cycle stylized facts. Looking at modern papers in this research field, the application of spectral analysis methods is rather the exception than the rule. What is the reason for this development?

As it will be shown in the following, the normally used spectral estimate, the periodogram, has serious drawbacks, especially for econometric purposes. But even if the periodogram was an appropriate estimate, other problems remain.

We face two major issues before we can apply spectral analysis to an economic time series. First, a stationary series is needed, i.e. a series for which the mean and the variance do not change over time. But most modern economic time series are not stationary, they exhibit a more or less obvious trend. Before the spectrum of the series can be computed, the nature of the non-stationarity has to be examined, and then, the series has to be transformed in an appropriate way in order to achieve stationarity. 'Appropriate' means in this context that the cyclical structure of the series should not be distorted, i.e. one has to avoid the problem of spurious cycles. This issue will be discussed in detail in Appendix A.

The second problem one faces in the application of spectral analysis to economic time series is the short observation period. The classical spectral estimate is not suitable for short data records for reasons discussed in Section 3.3 on p. 70. This problem can be solved to a large extent by computing the autoregressive spectrum (AR-spectrum), as advocated by Akaike (1969) and Parzen (1974).

Burg (1967) showed that the AR spectral estimate can be derived from the Maximum Entropy (ME-) approach, which leads to an estimate based on much more reasonable assumptions than the periodogram. This method was already applied fruitfully to the description of business cycle stylized facts.[1]

In the following, the spectral measures used in this study are explained (Section 3.2). Moreover, the differences between classical spectral estimation and ME spectral analysis are discussed (Section 3.3).

3.2   Spectral Measures

In this section, a more detailed overview of the spectral measures used in the study is given.[2] The easiest way to get familiar with the interpretation of the spectrum is to look at the *Cramér representation* of a time series model. Consider the model[3]

$$X_t = \sum_{j=1}^{n} \left(a_j \cos\left(\omega_j t\right) - b_j \sin\left(\omega_j t\right) \right);$$ (3.1)

where a_j and b_j are random components with following properties:

---

[1] See Hillinger and Sebold-Bender (1992) for a number of OECD countries, Reiter (1995), Part II for the United States and Germany, and Woitek (1996) for the G7-countries.

[2] See e.g. Brockwell and Davis (1991), pp. 434-443, Priestley (1981), vol. II, and Koopmans (1974), pp. 119-164.

[3] The following can be found in Harvey (1993), pp. 175-179, and Granger and Newbold (1986), pp. 48-53.

$$
\begin{aligned}
\mathrm{E}\,[a_j] &= \mathrm{E}\,[b_j] = 0; \; j = 1, \dots, n; \\
\mathrm{Var}\,[a_j] &= \mathrm{Var}\,[b_j] = \sigma_j^2; \; j = 1, \dots, n; \\
\mathrm{E}\,[a_j a_k] &= \mathrm{E}\,[b_j b_k] = 0; \; j \neq k; \\
\mathrm{E}\,[a_j b_k] &= 0 \; \forall \; k, j;
\end{aligned}
$$

Hence, the model consists of n superimposed harmonic waves for which the respective amplitude and phase are stochastic. For the covariance function, we have

$$
\begin{aligned}
\gamma(0) &= \sum_{j=1}^{n} \sigma_j^2; \\
\gamma(\tau) &= \sum_{j=1}^{n} \sigma_j^2 \cos\left(\omega_j \tau\right);
\end{aligned}
$$

We see that the process variance $\gamma(0)$ can be expressed as the sum of the variances σ_j^2 of the random components a_j and b_j.

In the above example, the number of frequencies is assumed to be finite. If we want to cover the case where all frequencies in the range $[0, \pi]$ are important, we have to extent the model in equation (3.1) allowing for a uncountably infinite number of frequency components:

$$
X_t = \int_0^\pi \cos\left(\omega t\right) da(\omega) + \int_0^\pi \sin\left(\omega t\right) db(\omega); \tag{3.2}
$$

The expression in equation (3.2) is the *spectral representation* or *Cramér representation* of a stochastic process. $a(\omega)$ and $b(\omega)$ are complex valued random variables. $da(\omega) = [a(\omega + d\omega) - a(\omega)]$ and $da(\omega) = [b(\omega + b\omega) - b(\omega)]$ have the following properties:

$$
\mathrm{E}[da(\omega)] = \mathrm{E}[db(\omega)] = 0;
$$

Hence, the expected value of X_t is zero. $da(\omega)$ and $db(\omega)$ are orthogonal and, in addition, cross orthogonal:

$$E[da(\omega)\ da(\omega')] \;=\; E[db(\omega)\ db(\omega')] = 0;\ \omega \neq \omega';$$

$$E[da(\omega)\ db(\omega')] \;=\; 0\ \forall\ \omega,\omega';$$

Let us now define the complex random variable

$$dz(\omega) = 0.5\left(da(\omega) + idb(\omega)\right);$$

Using this expression, equation (3.2) becomes

$$X_t = \int_{-\pi}^{\pi} e^{i\omega t} dz_x(\omega) \tag{3.3}$$

with[4]

$$E[dz_x(\omega)dz_x^\star(\omega')] \;=\; 0;\ \omega \neq \omega';$$
$$E[dz_x(\omega)dz_x^\star(\omega')] \;=\; f(\omega)d\omega;\ \omega = \omega';$$

where $f_x(\omega)$, a continuous function of ω, is called the *power spectrum* of the process $\{X_t\}$.[5] Equation (3.3) is the *complex spectral representation* of $\{X_t\}$, which is easier to handle than equation (3.2). The covariance function of $\{X_t\}$ is obtained by

$$\begin{aligned}
\gamma_x(\tau) \;=\; E[X_t X_{t-\tau}^\star] &= \int_{-\pi}^{\pi}\int_{-\pi}^{\pi} e^{i\omega t} e^{-i\omega(t-\tau)} E[dz_x(\omega)dz_x^\star(\omega')] \;= \\
&= \int_{-\pi}^{\pi} e^{i\omega t\tau} f(\omega)d\omega; \\
\gamma_x(0) &= \int_{-\pi}^{\pi} f_x(\omega)d\omega;
\end{aligned} \tag{3.4}$$

$$f_x(\omega) = \frac{1}{2\pi}\sum_{\tau=-\infty}^{\infty} \gamma_x(\tau)e^{-i\omega\tau};\ -\pi \le \omega \le \pi; \tag{3.5}$$

---

[4] The superscript '*' denotes the complex conjugate transpose.
[5] For the sake of convenience, the spectrum is expressed as a function of the radians ω; $\omega = 2\pi\lambda$; $\lambda \in [-0.5, 0.5]$. In Section 2, the spectra were plotted against λ in order to make it easier to derive the respective cycle lengths from the graphics.

From these expressions the interpretation of the spectrum $f_x(\omega)$ becomes apparent: The area under the power spectrum equals the process variance $\gamma_x(0)$, $f(\omega)d\omega$ being the part of the variance of $\{X_t\}$ that is due to the component $X_t(\omega)$ with frequencies in the interval $[\omega, \omega + d\omega]$. A peak at the frequency ω means that the respective component contributes a large part to the process variance, low values of $f_x(\omega)$ indicate that the contribution to the variance is small.

In the following, the normalized power spectrum is used, i.e. the power spectrum $f_x(\omega)$ is divided by the process variance $\gamma_x(0)$:

$$\tilde{f}_x(\omega) = \frac{f_x(\omega)}{\gamma_x(0)}; \tag{3.6}$$

Hence, the area under the normalized power spectrum equals one. Now assume that the autospectrum $f_x(\omega)$ has a peak at the frequency ω^*. Since the spectrum is a continuous function of ω, the part of the variance which can be explained by a harmonic wave with frequency ω^* has to be computed as part of the area under the normalized power spectrum in an appropriate intervall around the peak frequency ω^*. In this study, the frequency intervall of $\pm 0.1\omega^*$ is used to compute the *peak power* (*pp*), following a suggestion by C. Hillinger.

$$pp(\omega^*) = \frac{2}{\gamma_x(0)} \int_{\omega^*-0.1\omega^*}^{\omega^*+0.1\omega^*} f_x(\omega)d\omega \tag{3.7}$$

This expression can be interpreted similarily to R^2 in a regression model. The higher $pp(\omega^*)$, the more important is the cycle with frequency ω^* for the cyclical structure of the series (Figure 3.1 on the next page).

Fig. 3.1: Peak Power

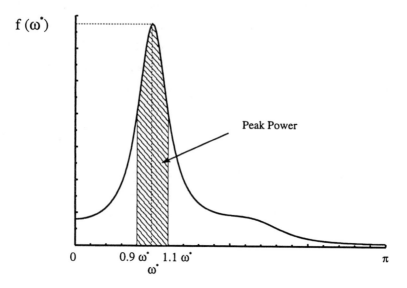

A measure to judge the spread of a peak, i.e the damping of a cycle, is the *bandwidth* (Figure 3.2 on the facing page), i.e. the range over which the amplitude of the respective cycle is reduced by one half: The sharper the peak at a frequency ω^*, the smaller the bandwidth.[6] The bandwidth has the disadvantage that it cannot be computed if the respective cycle is too strongly damped or if two peaks are too close. Therefore, it is more informative to look at the moduli of the corresponding complex roots of the characteristic polynomial used to estimate the univariate spectrum as explained below.

---

[6] See Priestley 1981, pp. 513-517.

Fig. 3.2: Bandwidth

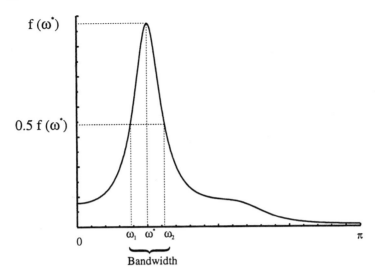

Another important measure is the *signal-to-noise ratio*. It measures the influence of the noise on a series and is defined as the ratio of the variance of the signal to the variance of the noise.

$$SNR = \frac{\int_{-\omega}^{\omega} f_x(\omega)d\omega - \sigma_{u_x}^2}{\sigma_{u_x}^2}; \qquad (3.8)$$

Assume now a second stationary process $\{Y_t\}$ which has the complex spectral representation

$$Y_t = \int_{-\pi}^{-\pi} e^{i\omega t} dz_y(\omega);$$

For the two processes $\{X_t\}$ and $\{Y_t\}$ the following additional property is needed:

$$\gamma_{xy}(\tau) = E[X_t Y_{t-\tau}] = \gamma_{yx}(-\tau);$$

i.e. the cross-covariance function is time independent, which requires

$$E[dz_x(\omega)dz_y^*(\omega')] = 0; \ \omega \neq \omega';$$

The *cross spectrum* is given by

$$f_{xy}(\omega) = \frac{1}{2\pi} \sum_{\tau=-\infty}^{+\infty} \gamma_{xy}(\tau) e^{-i\omega\tau} = c_{xy}(\omega) - i q_{xy}(\omega); \qquad (3.9)$$

where $c_{xy}(\omega)$ is the *cospectrum* and $q_{xy}(\omega)$ is the *quadrature spectrum*. From the co- and the quadrature spectrum of two series it is possible to compute measures for the lead-lag relationships between them. These measures are the *phase lag*, the *gain* and the *squared coherency*. Let us begin with the squared coherency:

$$|\kappa_{xy}(\omega)|^2 = \frac{|f_{xy}(\omega)|^2}{f_x(\omega) f_y(\omega)}; \qquad (3.10)$$

The cross covariance function can be written as

$$\gamma_{xy}(\tau) = E[X_t Y_{t-\tau}^\star] = \int_{-\pi}^{\pi} \int_{-\pi}^{\pi} e^{i\omega t} e^{-i\omega(t-\tau)} E[dz_x(\omega) dz_y^\star(\omega')] =$$
$$= \int_{-\pi}^{\pi} e^{i\omega\tau} f_{xy}(\omega) d\omega;$$

Hence,

$$E[dz_x(\omega) dz_y^\star(\omega')] = f_{xy}(\omega) d\omega;$$

and equation (3.9) can be written as

$$|\kappa_{xy}(\omega)|^2 = \frac{E[dz_x(\omega) dz_y^\star(\omega)]}{E[dz_x(\omega) dz_x^\star(\omega)] E[dz_y(\omega) dz_y^\star(\omega)]};$$

We see that $|\kappa_{jk}(\omega)|^2$ is the squared correlation coefficient of $dz_x(\omega)$ and $dz_y(\omega)$. It satisfies the inequalities $0 \leq |\kappa_{jk}(\omega)|^2 \leq 1, \omega \in [-\pi, \pi]$; and the measure can be interpreted in the same way as the correlation coefficient in a regression model. It measures the degree of linear relationship between a cycle of frequency ω in the series j and a cycle of the same frequency in the series k. If it equals 1 at a frequency ω, there is an exact linear relationship between the cycles with frequency ω in the two series; if it equals 0, there is no relationship between the two cycles.

If one writes equation (3.9) in polar coordinates, one obtains

$$f_{xy}(\omega) = \alpha_{xy}(\omega)e^{i\phi_{xy}(\omega)};\tag{3.11}$$

where

$$\alpha_{xy}(\omega) = \sqrt{c_{xy}(\omega)^2 + q_{xy}(\omega)^2};\tag{3.12}$$

is called the *amplitude spectrum* and

$$\phi_{xy}(\omega) = -\arctan(q_{xy}(\omega)/c_{xy}(\omega));\tag{3.13}$$

is called the *phase spectrum*.[7] The *gain spectrum* is defined as

$$g_{xy}(\omega) = \frac{\alpha_{xy}(\omega)}{f_{xy}(\omega)};\tag{3.14}$$

If we write equation (3.14) as

$$g_{xy}(\omega) = \frac{\sqrt{E[dz_x(\omega)dz_y^*(\omega)]}}{E[dz_y(\omega)dz_y^*(\omega)]};$$

it can be seen that the gain is the regression coefficient of a component $X_t(\omega)$ on the corresponding component $Y_t(\omega)$. In other words, the gain measures the multiplicative change of the amplitude of a cycle if transformed from series Y to series X. The phase spectrum measures the (average) phase lead of the series X over the series Y at a frequency ω.

---

[7] For the definition of q_{xy} and c_{xy}, see equation (3.9).

AR and VAR Processes

An AR process of order p (AR(p)-process) is defined as[8].

$$X_t = \alpha_1 X_{t-1} + \alpha_2 X_{t-2} + \cdots + \alpha_p X_{t-p} + u_t; \qquad (3.15)$$

where $\{u_t\}$ follows a white noise process with mean 0 and variance σ^2. In lag operator notation, we have

$$A(L)X_t \;=\; u_t;$$
$$A(L) \;=\; 1 - \alpha_1 L - \alpha_2 L^2 - \cdots - \alpha_p L^p;$$
$$L^n X_t \;=\; X_{t-n}; \; n \in \mathbb{Z};$$

i.e. the $\{u_t\}$ can be represented as output of a linear filter $A(L)$ which is applied to an AR-process $\{X_t\}$. If all zeros of the characteristic polynomial

$$1 - \alpha_1 z - \alpha_2 z^2 - \cdots - \alpha_p z^p = 0; \qquad (3.16)$$

are outside the unit circle, the process is stationary, i.e. it has a constant mean μ (in our case, $\mu = 0$) and a covariance function $\gamma(\tau); \tau = 0, 1, \ldots$ which is only dependent on the lag τ but not on the time t.[9]

If the process $\{X_t\}$ is stationary, it can be represented as output of a linear filter $A(L)^{-1}$ applied to the white noise process $\{u_t\}$:

$$X_t = A(L)^{-1} u_t;$$

The spectrum of the AR(p)-process is given by

---

[8] For the following see e.g. Priestley (1981), pp. 114-135, Brockwell and Davis (1991), pp. 122-125, Harvey (1993), pp. 179-181, Lütkepohl (1991), pp. 9-27.

[9] Since $\gamma(\tau)$ is an even function (i.e. $\gamma(\tau) = \gamma(-\tau)$), it is sufficient to look at it at lags $\tau \geq 0$.

$$f(\omega) \;=\; A(\omega)^{-1}\sigma^2 = \frac{1}{2\pi}\frac{\sigma^2}{\left|1 - \displaystyle\sum_{j=1}^{p} \alpha_j e^{-i\omega j}\right|^2};$$

(3.17)

$$-\pi \le \omega \le \pi;$$

where $A(\omega)$ is the Fourier transform of the filter $A(L)$.

An n-dimensional VAR-process of order p (VAR(p)-process) is defined as

$$\mathbf{X}_t = \mathbf{A}_1\mathbf{X}_{t-1} + \mathbf{A}_2\mathbf{X}_{t-2} + \cdots + \mathbf{A}_p\mathbf{X}_{t-p} + \mathbf{u}_t;$$

(3.18)

$\{\mathbf{u}_t\}$ is an n-dimensional white noise process with covariance matrix Σ_u and mean $\mathbf{0}$, $\mathbf{X}_t$ is a $(n \times 1)$ random vector, and the parameter matrices $\mathbf{A}_j; j = 1, \ldots, p$ are fixed $(n \times n)$ matrices. In lag operator notation we have

$$\begin{aligned}\mathbf{A}(L)\mathbf{X}_t &= \mathbf{u}_t;\\ \mathbf{A}(L) &= \mathbf{I} - \mathbf{A}_1 L - \mathbf{A}_2 L^2 - \ldots - \mathbf{A}_p L^p;\end{aligned}$$

The $(n \times n)$-spectral denstiy matrix $\mathbf{F}(\omega)$ is given by

$$\begin{aligned}\mathbf{F}(\omega) &= \tfrac{1}{2\pi}\mathbf{A}(\omega)_p^{-1}\Sigma_u\mathbf{A}(\omega)_p^{-*};\\ \mathbf{A}(\omega) &= \mathbf{I} - \mathbf{A}_1 e^{-i\omega} - \mathbf{A}_2 e^{-i2\omega} - \ldots - \mathbf{A}_p e^{-ip\omega};\end{aligned}$$

(3.19)

$$-\pi \le \omega \le \pi;$$

where the superscript '*' denotes the complex conjugate transpose of $\mathbf{A}(\omega)$.

3.3   The Maximum-Entropy Spectrum

As mentioned in the introduction at the beginning of Chapter 2, the periodogram, has serious drawbacks if applied to the very short macroeconomic
time series we have to do with. To understand the reason why it is useful to
look at the definition of the univariate periodogram.

In Chapter 2 it was stated that the periodogram can be obtained by fitting
harmonic waves to a stationary series at a set of frequencies λ_j (*Fourier
frequencies*) and computing R^2 for each wave. The periodogram can be
looked upon as the Fourier transform of the sample autocovariance function
(see equation 2.4 on p. 32).

One of the interpretation problems becomes now apparent: While the
true spectrum of a series is continuous, the periodogram is discrete, since
it is defined only at the Fourier frequencies. In addition, we face special
problems applying the periodogram to economic time series. These problems
are summarized in a critical remark by Mitchell (1927), pp. 259-261, which,
in my opinion, is a very good description of the situation. Therefore, the
entire passage is cited here despite of its length:

> To readers trained in the natural sciences, it may seem that pe-
> riodogram analysis should be substituted for the cumbersome and
> inexact procedure which has been described as the standard method
> of determining cyclical fluctuations. [...] It yields excellent results
> in many physical processes which show strictly periodic fluctua-
> tions of a symmetrical type, and it should reveal any similar peri-
> odicities which exist in economic time series. Nor is the method
> limited to the discovery of simple movements. A periodogram
> analysis may indicate the existence of several or many periodici-
> ties, which when combined with each other give a curve so compli-
> cated that the uninitiated reader would not suppose it to be made
> up of periodic elements. Perhaps it will be found that many of the
> time series used by the business-cycle statisticians can be usefully
> described by " synthetic curves" formed by adding together several
> periodic fluctuations which differ in length.
>
> But the systematic application of periodogram analysis to eco-
> nomic series encounters serious obstacles. [...]

> *The most obvious of these obstacles to the systematic use of the
> periodogram method in business-cycle work - the brevity of the
> majority of the series which must be analyzed - presumably will
> shrink with the lapse of time. If the future is less checkered by
> catastrophes than the past has been, the troubles caused by irreg-
> ular fluctuations will diminish also. The doubts now harbored
> about the propriety of adjusting series to get rid of trends and
> seasonal fluctuations before beginning periodogram analysis may
> be set at rest by further work. [...] Certainly we cannot say that
> periodogram analysis will not play a large rôle in future economic
> work. But it seems equally certain that we cannot yet make it the
> standard procedure for studying cyclical fluctuations.*

Given today's situation, the view of Mitchell seems rather optimistic.
The series to be analyzed in macroeconometrics are still rather short, and
the problem of detrending without causing artificial cycles is still debated.
This question will be discussed in Appendix A; in this section, a possible
solution for the first problem, the short observation period, is presented.

What is the reason for the periodogram to be only a a poor estimate for
the theoretical spectrum?[10] First, the periodogram is an inconsistent though
unbiased estimate, because the variance does not vanish with increasing sample size. This is due to the cumulative effect of the variances of the sample
autocovariances in equation (2.4): "[T]*he reason why* [the variance of the
periodogram] *does not tend to zero is because, loosely speaking, it contains
'too many' sample autocovariances*" (Priestley (1981), p. 432).

Moreover, the empirical autocovariances are only known in the observation period. To estimate the spectrum using the classical approach it is
simply assumed that the autocovariances outside the sample are zero. There
are a huge number of spectra which are compatible with the sample autocovariances. One cannot expect that to choose out of this set of possible
spectra that almost certainly wrong spectrum for which the underlying au-
tocovariance function is zero for $|\tau| \geq N$ will lead to a good estimate of the
true spectrum (see Jaynes (1985), p. 39). With a small sample, this problem

---

[10] See Priestley (1981), pp 432-449.

becomes even more important.

These reasons lead to the difficulties in interpreting the periodogram of a short time series. But even with longer time series, the periodogram is an inconsistent estimate for the true spectrum. In order to decide whether a peak in the periodogram is spurious or not, one has to take into account effects like leakage, aliasing and harmonics (see e.g. Bloomfield (1976)). Smoothing the periodogram using spectral windows like the Bartlett-window or the Priestley-window leads to consistent estimates, but other problems appear.[11]

To show this, consider the following very simple example of the application of a spectral window, the *truncated periodogram*:

$$\tilde{I}(\lambda) = \frac{1}{2\pi} \sum_{\tau=-(N-1)}^{N-1} h(\tau)\hat{\gamma}(\tau)e^{-i2\pi\lambda\tau};$$

(3.20)

$$h(\tau) = \begin{cases} 1 & \text{if } |\tau| \leq M \\ 0 & \text{if } |\tau| > M \end{cases};$$

The sample autocovariance function has the weight '1' if the lag $|\tau|$ is less than or equal to M; $M < (N-1)$ and '0' otherwise. We see that after one has chosen the appropriate window type, one has to decide which maximum lag M to take. For both decisions, a number of criteria is described in e.g. Koopmans (1974), pp. 308-309, and Priestley (1981), pp 502-504. The choice of the appropriate window type seems not to be too difficult, since the differences are very clear. But this is not true for the determination of M. If prior knowledge on the form of the true spectrum is available, it is possible to determine M as a function of the sample size N and the minimum bandwidth B_{min}, which is required to reproduce the overall shape of the true spectrum (see Priestley (1981), pp. 517-520).

---

[11] Applying a spectral window means to assign different weights to the sample autocovariances dependent on the magnitude of the lag τ (see e.g the overview in Kay (1988), pp. 63-99).

*Without such knowledge there is no method of constructing esti-
mates which satisfy well defined objective criteria. [...] it must be
admitted that there are many situations in which we have no prior
knowledge whatsoever on the spectral bandwidth. Unfortunately,
these occur only too frequently in practice; for example, in the
analysis of economic time series where the concept of bandwidth
does not have any obvious physical interpretation. In such cases
one may still attempt to estimate spectral density functions but
now we have to adopt more of a 'trial and error' approach to the
selection of the estimation parameters.* (Priestley (1981), p. 538)

Now the problem arises that the smaller M, the smaller the variance
of the estimate, but the higher the bias, i.e. one faces a trade-off between
resolution and precision[12]. Looking at procedures suggested in the literature
to solve this dilemma one sees that the methods are quite arbitrary, which
might be fatal in some situations. In the multivariate case, one has to face
similar problems. Burg (1975), p. X, gives the following summary of the
above discussed issue:

*If one were not blinded by the mathematical elegance of the con-
ventional approach, making unfoundend assumptions as to the
values of unmeasured data* [by assuming that the autocovariances
are zero outside the sample, U.W.] *and changing the data values that one knows* [by assigning weights to the autocovariances
inside the sample, U.W.] *would be totally unacceptable from a
common sense and, hopefully, from a scientific point of view.*

As said before, the defects of the periodogram are mainly due to the assumption that the autocovariance function outside the observation period is
0. One might expect that the estimate becomes more reliable if it is based
on a more reasonable assumption. We are searching for a spectral estimate
which is compatible with the sample autocovariances, and we do not know
anything about the out-of-sample autocovariance function. This is exactly
the problem which is solved by the application of the *Maximum Entropy*

---

[12] This is the uncertainty principle of Grenander (1958), p. 155: *"Resolvability (bandwidth,
bias) and statistical reliability are antagonistic."*

(ME-) principle (or First Principle of Data Reduction) to spectral analysis, which was initiated by Burg ((1967), (1968), (1975)). The ME-principle was developed by Shannon and Jaynes[13] and can be stated as follows (Ables 1974, p 23):

> *The result of any transformation imposed on the experimental data shall incorporate and be consistent with all relevant data and be maximally non-committal with regard to unavailable data.*

In practice, one maximizes an entropy measure, i.e. a measure of 'non-knowledge', subject to the restriction that the result must be compatible with the sample information. This means that we have to look for that stationary time series which " *is the most random or least predictable time series that is consistent with the measurements.*" (Burg 1975, p.1). In the following, this principle will be applied to the multivariate case.

To derive the $(n \times n)$ ME-spectral density matrix, we have to solve the following maximization problem:

$$\max_{\mathbf{F}(\lambda)} \int_{-\pi}^{\pi} \ln\left(|\mathbf{F}(z)|\right) d\omega; \, z = e^{-i\omega}; \tag{3.21}$$

which is the measure for the entropy, subject to the $(2p+1)n^2$ restrictions

$$\int_{-\pi}^{\pi} \mathbf{F}(z) z^{\tau} d\omega = \Gamma(-\tau); \, \tau = 0, \pm 1, \ldots, \pm p; \tag{3.22}$$

given that it is possible to measure the autocovariance function up to the maximum lag p. Using the Lagrange multiplier method to solve this variational problem, Burg (1975), pp. 73-77, shows that the solution takes the form

$$\mathbf{F}(\omega)_A = \frac{1}{2\pi} \mathbf{A}(\omega)_p^{-1} \Sigma_p^f \mathbf{A}(\omega)_p^{-*}; \tag{3.23}$$

---

[13] See the overview in Jaynes (1985).

$A(\omega)_p$ is the Fourier transform of a forward prediction filter of order p, and Σ_p^f is the prediction error covariance matrix. The parameter matrices of the filter are determined by the following equation system:

$$
\begin{pmatrix}
\Gamma(0) & \Gamma(-1) & \cdots & \Gamma(-p) \\
\Gamma(1) & \Gamma(0) & \cdots & \vdots \\
\vdots & & \ddots & \Gamma(1) \\
\Gamma(p) & & \Gamma(1) & \Gamma(0)
\end{pmatrix}
\begin{pmatrix}
I_n \\
A_1 \\
\vdots \\
A_p
\end{pmatrix}
=
\begin{pmatrix}
\Sigma_p^f \\
0 \\
\vdots \\
0
\end{pmatrix}
;
\tag{3.24}
$$

which is formally identical to the Yule-Walker equations of a VAR(p)-process. The spectral density matrix for the forward prediction error filter is formally identical to the spectral density matrix of a VAR(p)-process as defined in equation (3.19). In the univariate case, the ME-spectrum takes the form

$$
f(\omega) = \frac{1}{2\pi} \frac{\sigma^2}{\left| 1 + \sum_{j=1}^{p} a_1 e^{-i\omega j} \right|^2};
\tag{3.25}
$$

where the a_j are the parameters of a forward (or backward) prediction error filter of order p. The parameters σ^2; a_j; $j = 1, \dots, p$ are determined by an equation system which is formally identical to the extended Yule-Walker equations. A more detailed description of the derivation of the univariate ME-spectrum can be found in e.g. Burg (1975), pp. 8-13, Geyer (1985), pp. 82-85, and Sebold-Bender (1990), pp. 35-41.

3.4   Parameter Estimation

Until recently, a 'second-best solution' was applied in the empirical work at SEMECON to the univariate and multivariate estimation of AR-models. The estimation algorithms were based on the fact that in the frequency domain, the direction of time is not important. To use as much information as possible as possible from the short data records, the parameters were estimated by minimizing both the forward- and the backward-prediction error.[14] For short observation periods, this method proved to be superior to the normally used Yule-Walker or OLS-method (see Swingler (1979)) in terms of resolution of the resulting spectra. All of these methods are approximative Maximum-Likelihood (ML) estimates, and were recommended in the literature because of the time consuming task of ML-estimation.[15] In this study, the parameters of the AR-models were estimated applying full information maximum likelihood. The likelihood function was recursively computed following the Kalman-filter approach (see e.g. Harvey (1992)).

An important problem in the estimation of AR-models is the choice of the maximum lag p. For the description of business cycle stylized facts, one is basically interested to find the lowest possible order which is capable to reproduce the cyclical structure of the series, i.e. an order which produces the appropriate number of conjugate complex roots in the characteristic polynomial. In this study, the univariate and multivariate version of the BAC-criterion recently developed by Heintel (1994) is applied. This criterion is based on the framework of Bayesian time series analysis. The BAC is preferable to the widely used information criteria from a theoretical point of view, because these methods determine the order by minimizing the sum of the estimated error variance and a more or less arbitrary penalty term, and prior information can be taken into account in a way which is replicable. As simulation studies have shown, the BAC is also preferable from a more practical view, because it results in more robust order estimates.

---

[14] In the univariate case, the *Burg algorithm* (Burg (1975)) or alternatively the *Fougere algorithm* (Fougere (1985)) were used. In the multivariate case, the *Vieira-Morf algorithm* (Morf, Vieira, Lee and Kailath (1978)) was applied. For a detailed description and application examples see Sebold-Bender (1990), Sebold-Bender (1992), Hillinger and Sebold-Bender (1992), Reiter (1995), pp. 20-49, and Woitek (1996).

[15] See e.g. Marple (1987), p. XVIII, or Kay (1988), pp. 217-220.

Part II

Empirical Results

Chapter 4

Business Cycle Stylized Facts
in the OECD Countries

4.1   Overview

In the following sections, I analyze the cyclical structure of prices and money
stock (M1) in addition to the GDP and its components.[1] As stated above,
the business cycle stylized facts of these series are analyzed in the modern
literature focussing on the following basic aspects: (1) The amplitude of
the fluctuations; and (2) the degree of comovement with a measure for the
output, together with the phase shift of the series relative to the output cycle.
Lucas (1977), p. 218 summarizes the commonly accepted view concerning
these aspects:

---

[1] It would be interesting to examine the cyclical structure of other series playing an
important role in business cycle models as well, such as the unemployment rate, or
short-term and long-term interest rates. But since the historical data set of Backus and
Kehoe (1992), which I use as a basis for comparison, does not contain other series, I
restrict the analysis in this way in order to make the results comparable.

The programs used in this chapter are written in GAUSS and are based on procedures
developed by Monika Sebold-Bender and Rudolf Köhne-Volland.

> *There is, as far as I know, no need to qualify these observations by restricting them to particular countries or time periods: they appear to be regularities common to all decentralized market economies. Though there is absolutely no theoretical reason to anticipate it, one is led by the facts to conclude that, with respect to the qualitative behavior of co-movements among series,* business cycles are all alike. *To theoretically inclined economists, this conclusion should be attractive and challenging, for it suggests the possibility of a unified explanation of business cycles, rather than in political or institutional characteristics specific to particular countries or periods.*

Lucas claims that there are no country specific business cycle characteristics. Moreover, there are no significant changes in the cyclical pattern over time. In the following sections, results available from the literature are compared with business cycle stylized facts obtained from Maximum Entropy (ME-) spectral estimation to examine whether this view is justified.

First, an overview over some findings from the literature on business cycle stylized facts in the postwar period are presented. In Sections 4.2.1 and 4.2.2, this set of stylized facts is compared with business cycle characteristics for 11 OECD countries applying the spectral analysis technique described in Chapter 2. In Section 4.3 the univariate and multivariate business cycle stylized facts of macroeconomic time series in the prewar period (1870-1914) are analyzed.

Results from the Literature

In the main part of the empirical studies analyzing economic fluctuations, time domain methods are prevailing, such as those discussed in Chapter 2. As was shown there, these methods give only a rough impression of business cycle characteristics. Besides the methods in the time and the frequency domain presented in the previous sections, another technique to describe the characteristics of the business cycle can be found in the literature. This is the method of the National Bureau of Economic Research (NBER) going back to Burns and Mitchell (1946).[2] From a number of leading, coincident and lagging indicators, a measure for the genereal business cycle is constructed, with which it is possible to identify the turning points of the cycle. From these the average duration of the business cycle can be derived. Moreover, by comparing the turning points of the cycles in the specific series with the general business cycle, we are able to describe the lead-lag structure between them. The widely used results can be found in the NBER reference chronologies of business cycle peaks and troughs (see e.g. Moore and Zarnowitz (1986)).[3]

An example for the NBER-method can be found in the often cited study on business cycle characteristics by Zarnowitz (1985).[4] He finds for the duration of US business cycles (1854-1982) an average length of about 4 years.[5] Looking at the components of aggregate output, we see that consumption and fixed investment are roughly coincident with the general business cycle, while changes in inventories are leading with a phase shift of about 4-11 months (at seven business cycle peaks, 1948-80).[6]

The NBER-Methodology has been subjected to severe criticism because

---

[2] For an overview over the history and development of the NBER-methodology for the measurement of business cycles, see Moore and Zarnowitz (1986).

[3] An example for a recent application of the business cycle characteristics determined by the NBER can be found in Hamilton (1989). He estimates the probability that U.S. real GNP (1952-1984) is in contraction, respectively in expansion using a model for changes in regime. He compares the result with the NBER-business cycle, and finds a striking similarity.

[4] Together with related work on business cycles, it is reprinted Zarnowitz (1992).

[5] Zarnowitz (1985), Table 1, p. 526.

[6] See Zarnowitz (1992), Table 10.4.

of the arbitraryness of the choice and the relative weight of the series to construct the business cycle indices.[7] Moreover, the results are even less specific than the information obtained by time series analysis methods in the time domain.

Let us now turn to studies applying time domain methods. In Maußner (1994), p. 17, Table A.III.1 an overview over more recent studies of business cylce stylized facts can be found. Along with other studies, he lists the papers of Hodrick and Prescott (1980), Kydland and Prescott (1990), Backus and Kehoe (1992), Blackburn and Ravn (1992), Brandner and Neusser (1992).

Hodrick and Prescott (1980) apply their filter to quarterly US data in the observation period 1950-1979, and describe the stylized facts using time domain techniques. They find that: (1) Investment and private consumption show higher correlations with output than governmental consumption. (2) The fluctuations in the monetary aggregates are positively correlated with output fluctuations. (3) The price level fluctuates countercyclically.

In Chapter 2, the procedure of Kydland and Prescott (1990) was applied to demonstrate the use of time domain methods in the description of the business cycle. In their study on US postwar business cycles,[8] they reproduce the result from Hodrick and Prescott (1980) that (1) prices fluctuate countercyclically. This is an important outcome for judging the validity of business cycle theories (p.17): "*We caution that any theory in which procyclical prices figure crucially in accounting for postwar business cycle fluctuations is doomed to failure.*" The finding is looked upon as a strong argument in favour of real business cycle models, which explain the business cycle as being supply side driven. If demand side shocks were responsible for the business cycle, one would expect the price level to be procyclical.[9] In addition to this important stylized fact, they find that (2) M1 is procyclical, while M2 leads

---

[7] The Burns/Mitchell-method led to the well known debate on "*Measurement without Theory*" intitialized by Koopmans (1947) (See e.g. the overview in Morgan (1990), pp. 51-56.

[8] Quarterly data, observation period 1954-1989.

[9] For a discussion of this point see Chadha and Prasad (1994).

over the output cycle. (3) The investment series and private consumption are procyclical. (4) Governmental consumption and net exports are counter-cyclical.

Backus and Kehoe (1992) analyze the business cycle stylized facts using time domain methods in the observation period 1870-1986 for Australia, Canada, Denmark, Germany, Italy, Japan, Norway, Sweden, the United Kingdom, and the United States. The period is divided in the prewar period (before World War I), the postwar period (after World War II), and the interwar period. The results for the prewar and the interwar period are not presented here, because they are discussed in detail in Section 4.3.

To make the annual series stationary they use the Hodrick-Prescott filter. For the postwar period, Backus and Kehoe (1992) have the following results: (1) Private consumption and investment are procyclical. Investment fluctuations have the greatest amplitude. (2) The trade balance and the price level are countercyclical. (3) In the money stock, no pattern can be found.

Blackburn and Ravn (1992) examine quarterly data (United Kingdom) in the time domain for the observation period 1956-1990. They apply the Hodrick-Prescott filter to achieve stationarity. Their main results are: (1) Private consumption, business fixed investment, inventory investment, and monetary aggregates are procyclical. (2) Net exports and the price level are countercyclical. (3) Governmental consumption does not exhibit any cyclical pattern.

Brandner and Neusser (1992) obtain slightly different results for the business cycle characteristics of Germany and Austria. They analyze quarterly data in the observation period 1960-1989 for Germany and 1964-1989 for Austria using quarterly data. Unlike Backus and Kehoe (1992) and Blackburn and Ravn (1992), they test their results for robustness using three types of data transformations: The Hodrick-Prescott filter, a difference filter, and a linear time trend. Their main results are: (1) Consumption and investment are procyclical. (2) The trade balance and the price level are countercyclical. (3) Governmental consumption is countercyclical in Austria, but uncorrelated with output in Germany. (4) Money supply is uncorrelated in Austria; The German money supply is countercyclical.[10]

Summing up the results so far, we have the following list of stylized facts for the postwar period:[11]

1. Investment fluctuations are above average.

2. Investment and private consumption are procyclical; for governmental consumption, there is no robust pattern.

3. Net exports and the price level are countercyclical.

4. Concerning the correlation of the monetary aggregates with the output cycle, no robust stylized fact can be identified based on the studies cited above.

As mentioned in the introduction, it is possible to be more precise concerning business cycle characteristics, dependent on the method of choice. This was already demonstrated in Chapter 2. In addition, I present two examples from the literature which apply spectral analysis methods to the description of business cylce stylized facts.

Englund, Persson and Svensson (1992) examine the Swedish business cycle in the period 1861-1988. This study is very interesting, because they apply a technique which is totally different from the other papers present in this section. After making the annual series stationary using the Hodrick-Prescott (HP-) filter as well as a difference filter,[12] they use, besides time domain techniques, classical cross-spectral analysis methods to describe the business cycle stylized facts. Their major findings are: (1) The HP filtered

---

[10] Comparable results for Germany and Austria can be found in Schebeck and Tichy (1984) and and Smeets (1992).

[11] For additional evidence on these business cycle characteristics in the G7-countries, see Fiorito and Kollintzas (1992).

[12] Moreover, they apply band-pass filters in the time and the frequency domain to the HP filtered series in order to isolate the business cycle components, which they define to have cycle lengths in the range 3-8 years (pp. 355-359).

output, investment, and consumption series exhibit peaks in the spectra at cycle lengths of about 13 years. For the difference filtered series, the peaks are in the range between 3 and 8 years. (2) At these cycle lengths, the coherences between the output and the component series are very high. Consumption and investment are procyclical.

Due to the limited availability of data over this long period, the authors analyze fewer series in their paper than the other studies. These findings are more precise than those obtained by the previously cited authors, insofar as the cycle length at which the correlation between the series under analysis is highest is identified, together with their relative importance in the respective series. Moreover, they present the results for different filtering methods, which gives an impression of the robustness.

Another example of the advantages of spectral analysis methods can be found in Hillinger and Sebold-Bender (1992). Comparing the description of data characteristics in the time domain with the application of univariate ME spectral estimation, they show that the use of the appropriate spectral estimate is indeed preferable. The series are made stationary applying a polynomial trend or a logistic trend. The order of the AR-model is estimated using the univariate version of the CAT-criterion. Hillinger and Sebold-Bender (1992), (pp. 107-108) present the following list of univariate stylized facts for the GDP and its components (24 OECD countries, annual data, 1960-1986):

SF1. The fluctuations are concentrated in the investment series - inventory investment (II) and gross fixed capital formation (GFCF). [...]

SF2. GFCF exhibits cycles in the range of six to ten years often superposed by a cycle longer than 12 years. II contains a typical two- to four-year cycle additional to the longer cycles.

SF3. The period of the cycles, as well as their relative importance, depend on the respective country. Neighbouring countries tend to have similar patterns.

SF4. The II are more affected by the noise than the GFCF.

SF5. The longer cycles are just slightly damped. They concentrate in a narrow frequency band.

SF6. The short cycle is strongly damped. The corresponding frequency band is essentially wider than for the longer cycles.

In the following sections, this list is extended to the stylized facts of fluctuations in M1 and prices applying ME-spectral estimation as described in Chapter 2. Moreover, the lead-lag relationships between these series, the output components and the agrregate output is analyzed using multivariate spectral analysis.

4.2 Postwar Period

4.2.1 Univariate Results

To check whether the results for Germany in Chapter 2 are country spe-
cific, I estimated the spectra for Australia (AUS), Canada (CAN), Denmark
(DNK), France (FRA), United Kingdom (GBR), (western) Germany (GER),
Italy (ITA), Japan (JPN), Norway (NOR), Sweden (SWE) and the United
States (USA). The series under analysis are: Gross Domestic Product (GDP),
Gross Fixed Capital Formation (GFCF), Inventories (II), Private Consump-
tion (CP), Governmental Consumption (CG), Exports (EX), Imports (IM),
Net Exports (NEX),[13] Prices (P),[14] and M1.[15] The observation period is
1960-1991, again with the exception of GER (1960-1989), with annual data.[16]

The data (in logs)[17] are made stationary by applying both the Hodrick-
Prescott (HP100)[18] filter and the difference filter. As it will be explained
in Chapter A, there is no reliable test available to judge the type of non-
stationarity of our series. Therefore, we face the problem that the results of
the univariate spectral estimation might be spurious, i.e. due to the chosen
detrending procedure. To check the robustness of the results, I therefore
decided to present the outcome for both filters.[19] For the interpretation it
is important to bear in mind that the detrended series must be looked upon
as percentage deviations from the trend, respectively, as growth rates in the

---

[13] The net exports are analyzed for the postwar period in addition to EX and IM to make
it possible to compare the results with those from the data set by Backus and Kehoe
(1992) for the postwar period, which contains only NEX. Of course, the analysis of the
influence of foreign trade on the business cycles is more detailed if we look at EX and
IM and not at their aggregate.

[14] GDP deflator at market prices.

[15] Long series for M1 without severe structural breaks due to changes in the definition
were only available for AUS, CAN, JPN, NOR, and USA.

[16] Data source: OECD Statistical Compendium, 1994. The reason for the decision to
analyze annual data is given in fn. 3 on p. 11.

[17] Since II and NEX are sometimes negative, I compare the fluctuations of these series in
levels, similar to the procedure in Chapter 2.

[18] HP100: Hodrick-Prescott filter with $\mu = 100$; see Appendix A.

[19] For a similar procedure, see Baxter and Stockman (1989) and Reiter (1995).

case of the difference filter.[20]

To make the interpretation of the results easier, the figures on p. 92 ff. contain summaries of the cycle lengths, the importance of the cycles, and the regularity of the fluctuations, which is measured by the signal-to-noise ratio (SNR). The importance of the cycles is represented by the peak power pp. Moreover, the modulus gives an impression of the damping of a cycle. An error-bar type plot is used to give a visual impression of the variation of the results.[21]

In Figure 4.1, the results for the length of the long cycle are displayed.[22] The HP100 filtered GDP and its components exhibit a long cycle with a median of about 8 years. For the difference filtered series, the median is smaller (about 7 years). The long cycle in the HP100 filtered P is slightly shorter than the GDP cycle (about 7 years); in the difference filtered P, i.e. the inflation rate, cyclical structure can only be detected for two countries (AUS and ITA). M1 exhibits a long cycle with a length of about 11 years for both filtering methods. In general we see that in the difference filtered series, the long cycle is less often found than in the HP-filtered series.

For the short cycle, the result is reverse (Figure 4.2 on p. 93). In this case, the cyclical structure of the difference filtered series is dominated by the short cycle, i.e. these cycle lengths are more often found than in the HP100 filtered series. The average cycle length is about 3-4 years, independent of the filtering method.

What can be said about the relative importance of the cyclical components for the structure of the fluctuations? The results for the long and

---

[20] This is of course not the case for the GDP/II- and the GDP/NEX-systems. Since the GDP-growth rates follow a negative trend in the observation period (see e.g. Figure 2.2 on p. 16), they are not stationary. Based on the visual impression, I substracted a linear time trend from the growth rates, assuming that the filtered series is I(0), which is plausible for macroeconomic time series (see e.g. Nelson and Plosser (1982)). For details, see Appendix A.

[21] The detailed results of the univariate spectral estimation can be found in Tables B.1 - B.16, Appendix B.1 on p. 166 ff.

[22] See p. 92. In the following, a 'long' cycle is defined as a cycle with a length more than or equal to 5 years. 'Short' cycles have a length less than 5 years.

the short cycle are displayed in Figure 4.3 and 4.4.[23] For the HP100 filtered
GDPs, we have the following outcome: The pp of the long cycle has a median
of 0.20, while for the short cycle it is only 0.14. Looking at the components
and the other series, it can be seen that the long cycle has the highest pp in
CP (0.30) and GFCF (0.26), while the short cycle is most important in II
(0.18). Given the results for the other countries, the relatively small pps of
the long cycle in the Australian and the Danish GFCF (0.08 an 0.09) are surprising. P and M1 exhibit similar results as the GDP-components: The long
cycle is more important for the cyclical structure than the short cycle. The
importance of the long cycle in M1 varies extremely: We have pps between
0.05 for AUS and 0.67 for NOR.

The question whether these results are robust can be answered if looking
at the outcome for the difference filtered series. We see that in general, the
pp for the long cycles decreases, while the pp for the short cycles increases.
For both the long and the short cycle, II is now the series with the highest
median (0.22 for the long cycle, 0.31 for the short cycle).

From the plot of the moduli in Figures 4.5 and 4.6 (p. 96 f.) similar information can be obtained: We know that the higher the modulus, the sharper
the peak in the spectrum, and the higher the pp of the respective cycle.[24] In
general, the moduli are higher for the long cycles. For the difference filtered
series, the moduli are in general lower than for the HP100 filtered data.

An impression of the importance of the regular component of the detrended series can be obtained from the signal-to-noise ratio (SNR). Looking
at the plot of the SNRs for the HP100 filtered GDP and its components in
Figure 4.7 on p. 98 we see that the medians vary between 6 and 12. The
fluctuations of IM, EX, II, and CG are less regular than the fluctuations in
GDP (8.45); the result for II is lowest (6.07). GFCF (12.23) and CP (12.44)
exhibit the most regular fluctuations. The other series show similar SNRs.
The HP100 filtered P has a relatively high SNR if compared with the GDP

---

[23] See p. 94 and p. 95.

[24] For example, the correlation coefficient between the medians of pp and the moduli of
the long cycle are about 0.7 for both filtering methods.

components (10.59). The median for M1 is 7.27. In general, the SNR is lower on average for the difference filtered series. The results for the GDP and its components vary between 5 and 8; II is now the component with the highest SNR (7.67). The above results are comparable with the findings for Germany in the previous chapter, with the exception of the cyclical structure in IM. The HP100 filtered German imports fluctuate more regularily (SNR=12.45) than the imports in the other countries (median: 6.11). The outcome for the difference filter is similar.

Summing up, OECD business cycles have the following univariate characteristics:

1. In the GDP and its components, a long and a short cycle can be found with lengths of 7-9 years and 3-4 years. The cycles in M1 are longer on average than the cycles in the GDP.

2. The cyclical structure in the GDP is dominated by the long cycle. In the component series, this long cycle is most important in GFCF and CP, while the short cycle is of higher importance for the cyclical structure of II. For the other GDP components, the long and the short cycle are as prominent as the respective GDP cycles. A similar result can be found for the HP100 filterd P. The importance of the long cycle in M1 varies considerably.

3. For the HP100 filtered series, GFCF and CP are the GDP-components which exhibit the most regular fluctuations, II is the most irregular series. If the series are difference filtered, II becomes the most regular series.

4. In general, these findings are robust, with the exception of P, for which the result is clearly dependent on the filtering method: The cyclical structure of the HP100-filtered P is similar to the GDP-cycles, while the inflation rate does not exhibit cycles at all.

The last point coincides with the findings in Reiter (1995), pp. 41-43. As he states, this outcome does not show that the price cycles are spurious, *"but is due to the fact that the differences of prices exhibit a rather complicated trend which is not captured by a straight line.*" He illustrates his statement by comparing the results with other detrending procedures, and concludes that it is justifed to use the HP100 filter.

The results above add evidence to the view that the GDP cycles can be looked upon as investment cycles, as it was explained for the German GDP and its components in Chapter 2.[25] Therefore we can expect that the multivariate analysis confirms the strong coherence between the GDP cycles and the respective cycles in the two investment series found for Germany.

---

[25] The only exception are the results for Australia and Denmark. In these countries, the cyclical structure in fixed investment is less obvious than for the others.

As far as Australia is concerned, this result coincides with the literature. Bowden and Martin (1992) compare the Australian business cycle structure with the US business cycle applying classical spectral analysis techniques to monthly data. They conclude that "[t]*he Australian business cycle is quite evidently a much more diffuse sort of structure than is that for the United States*" (p. 396).

Fig. 4.1: OECD, Univariate Results, Cycle Lengths, Long Cycle

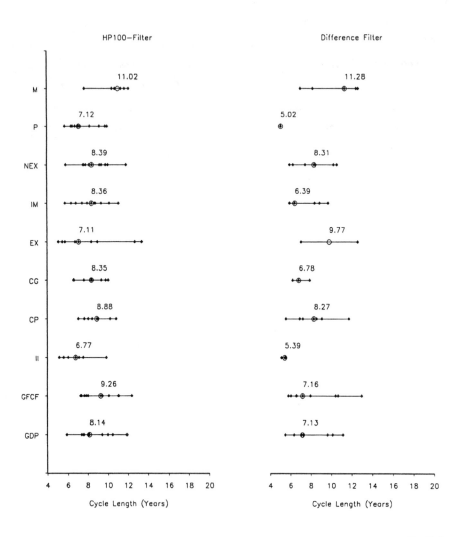

Cycle Length (Years)

Fig. 4.2: OECD, Univariate Results, Cycle Lengths, Short Cycle

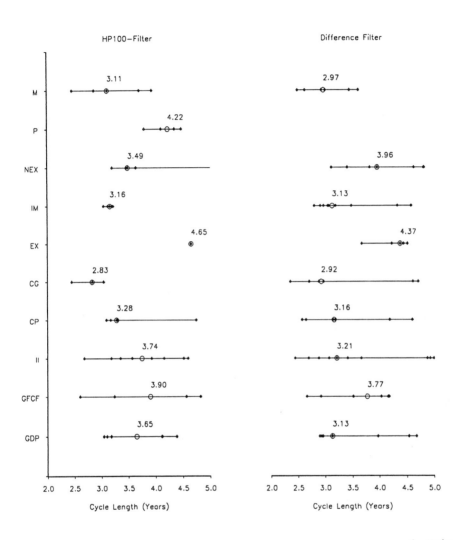

Fig. 4.3: OECD, Univariate Results, Peak Power (*pp*), Long Cycle

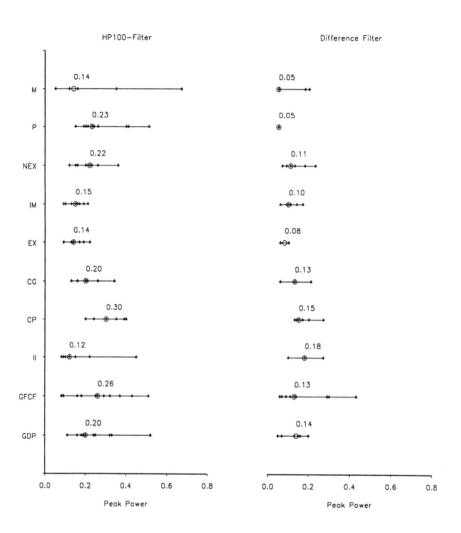

Fig. 4.4: OECD, Univariate Results, Peak Power (pp), Short Cycle

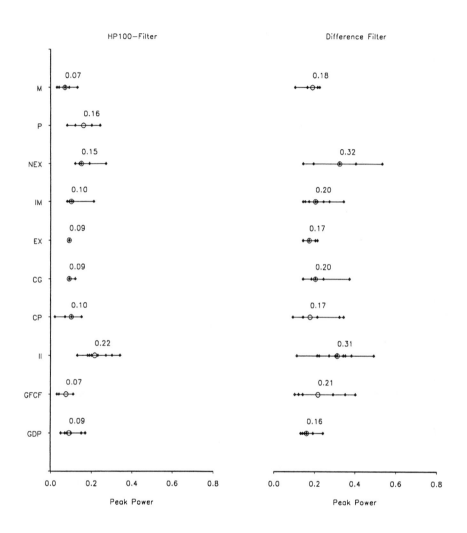

Fig. 4.5: OECD, Univariate Results, Modulus, Long Cycle

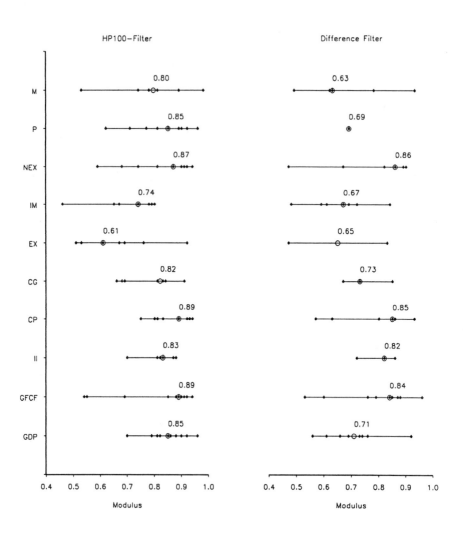

Fig. 4.6: OECD, Univariate Results, Modulus, Short Cycle

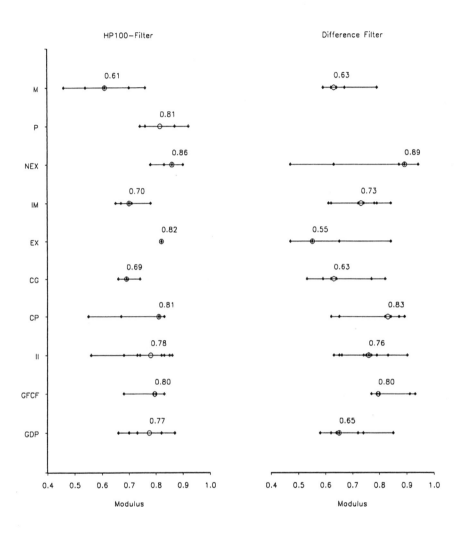

Fig. 4.7: OECD, Univariate Results, Signal-to-Noise Ratio (*SNR*)

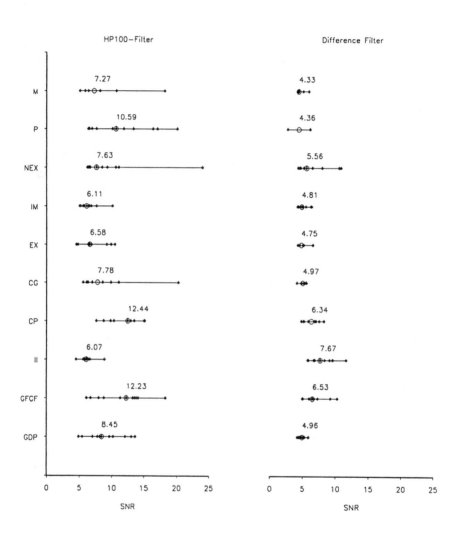

4.2.2   Multivariate Results

The results of the multivariate spectral estimation for the GDP and the other
series (squared coherency (sc), phase shift, gain) are displayed in Figure 4.8 -
4.13.[26] As in the most part of the literature, I compare the cyclical structure
of the component series, M1, and P with the respective GDP-cycles, although
an analysis of alterantive systems like M1/P would be important as well. The
measures are computed at the peak frequencies of the GDP-autospectrum;
as demonstrated in Chapter 2 for Germany, the results are very close to
the other possibilities (peak frequencies of the component spectrum, peak
frequencies of sc). The peak periods are not reported here, since they are
quite similar to the univariate results (see Chapter 2). There are a number of
series for which in the univariate case no cyclical structure could be detected.
Nevertheless, I decided to fit VAR-models to these series, too, following the
order recommended by the multivariate BAC-criterion.

The median of (sc) (Figure 4.8 and 4.9 on 103 ff.) is highest for the long
cycle in the HP100 filtered GDP/GFCF-system (0.88) and in the GDP/CP-
system (0.90). This result is robust; looking at the outcome for the difference filtered GDP components, we have for both the GDP/GFCF- and the
GDP/CP-system a median of 0.86. For IM, the result is slightly smaller
(HP100: 0.78; difference filter: 0.76). sc is lowest for the GDP/EX- (0.50)
and the GDP/CG-system (0.45), which is also the case for the difference
filtered series (0.69 and 0.40).

For the short cycle, the median of sc is highest in the GDP/II-system
(0.87), and lowest in the GDP/CG-system (0.19). The difference filtered
series exhibit again the highest median for the GDP/II-system (0.86), the
lowest in the GDP/EX-system (0.33).

The scs for the M1 are relatively low at both cycle lengths (HP100: 0.71,
0.52; difference filter: 0.42, 0.68). For P, we see that again the result is extremely sensitive to the detrending procedure: There is no coherence between

---

[26] Detailed results can be found in Tables B.9 - B.16 on p. 173 f.

the GDP growth rates and the inflation rate.

The results for the phase shift[27] in Figure 4.10 and 4.11 on p. 105 f. show that the long cycles in GFCF and CP are procyclical. In both cases, the median of the phase shift is less than 1 year (0.22 respectively 0.23 for the HP100 filtered series, 0.26 and 0.27 for the difference filtered series). The phase shift of the long cycle in II and CG is 1-2 years. As in the case of Germany in Chapter 2, IM is procyclical. Thus it has the expected dampening influence on the business cycle described above (Chapter 2). The long cycles in net exports are countercyclical with an absolute phase shift of about 3 years. The long cycle in the HP100 filtered P are also countercyclical, with the about the same absolute phase shift. The median of the absolute phase shift at the long cycle for M1 is less than one year, i.e. M1 fluctuates pro-cyclically. For the short cycle, similar results are obtained (Figure 4.3 on p. 94). In this case, the cycles in GFCF, II, CP as well as M1 are procyclical. The median of the absolute phase shift between the short cycle in GDP and CG is about 2 years. The same results are obtained for NEX and P.

From the sign of the results in Tables B.13 and B.14 on p. 177 f. we see that for both the HP100 filtered and the difference filtered series, the long cycle in II lags the long cycle in GDP as in the case of Germany, while it is not clear whether the long cycle in CG leads or lags the respective GDP cycle. The question whether the long cycles in M1 leads or lags the long GDP-cycle cannot be easily answered, But for 4 of 6 countries, the M1-cycle leads the long GDP cycle with a phase shift of about 2 years, both for the growth rates and the detrended series. (Tables B.13 and B.14 on p. 177 f.) Since we have only 6 M1 series available and the scs are relatively low, the result can hardly be looked upon as reliable. Together with the small sc s for the GDP cycles and the cycles in M1 and CG, this leads to the conclusion that there is no sign of an anticyclical fiscal or monetary policy in the postwar period.

---

[27] The absolute phase shift is displayed in the graphs because otherwise it would be difficult to get clear information from Figures 4.10 and 4.11.

In Figure 4.12 and 4.13,[28] the results for the gain of the long and the short cycles are displayed.[29] We see that in general, the amplitude of the cycles in the percentage deviations from the trend and in the growth rates are smaller for the GDP-cycles than for the cycles in the component series. The amplitudes in CP are only slightly smaller as the amplitudes of the long cycles in the GDP. The average gain is about 0.7-1, i.e. there is no change in the amplitude if the long CP cycle is transformed to the long cycle in GDP. The amplitudes of the long and the short cycles in the GDP are clearly smaller than the amplitudes of the respective cycles in fixed investment, IM, and EX (about 60 per cent).

From the results in the last two sections we see that in general, the stylized facts for the German GDP and its components as presented in Chapter 2 are not country specific. The business cycle characteristics of Germany can be extended to the following list of multivariate business cycle stylized facts for the 11 OECD countries in the postwar period (1960-1991):

1. Between the long GDP-cycles and the long GFCF-cycles, respectively between the short GDP-cycles and the short II-cycles, there is a strong relationship. Between the cyclical structure in the GDP and the cyclical structure in CG and EX the relationship is only weak.

2. If a long cycle can be found in II, it lags the respective GDP-cycle with a phase shift of about 1 year.

3. NEX and P are countercyclical.

4. The relationship between the cyclical structure in M1 and the GDP-cycles is only weak, both for the detrended series and the growth rates.

---

[28] See p. 107 and p. 108.
[29] The results for NEX and II are not in the graphics, because since the data are not in logs, the gain is not of the same order of magnitude as in the other cases. The outcome for the GDP/NEX- and the GDP/II-system, as well as the other results, can be found in Tables B.15 and B.16 on p. 179 f.

5. The amplitudes of the cycles in the GDP are smaller than the amplitudes of the respective cycles in the investment series.

In general, these findings are robust, with the exception of P. Again, P is the series for which the results strongly depend on the choice of the detrending procedure: For the GDP growth rates and the inflation rate, no multivariate cyclical structure could be found.[30]

The interpretation of the outcome for Germany in Chapter 2 is also valid for the above list of stylized facts. We have seen that the cycle in GDP has to be looked upon as investment cycle. The cycles in GDP have smaller amplitudes than the component cycles because of the smoothing effect of changes in inventories and the imports. Moreover, we have confirmed the result that prices fluctuate countercyclically; for the period and the countries under analysis, no sign of a countercyclical fiscal or monetary policy could be found.

After we have found the above set of robust stylized facts of business cycles between 1960 and 1991, the question arises whether they must be looked upon as typical for the postwar period. The cyclical structure of economic fluctuations in the last 200 years was a widely accepted fact among earlier business cycle theorists, as it is reported by Hicks (1950), p. 2.[31] Therefore, it will be an interesting next step to extend the previous analysis and apply ME-spectral estimation to historical macroeconomic time series.

---

[30] The finding that fluctuations in the prices are countercyclical in the postwar period corresponds to the results in the literature discussed above. The last point, i.e. the dependence of the result for the prices from the chosen detrending method, can also be found in Chadha and Prasad (1994). They analyze the cyclical behaviour of prices and output for the G7-countries (postwar quarterly data in logs) using time domain methods. Comparing different detrending procedures, they find for both the Hodrick-Prescott filter and the difference filter that prices are countercyclical. But the correlations between the inflation rate and the GDP growth rate are significantly smaller than for the detrended series.

[31] See also the citation of Lucas in the introduction of this chapter, p. 80.

Fig. 4.8: OECD, Multivariate Results, Long Cycle, Maximum Squared Coherency (*sc*)

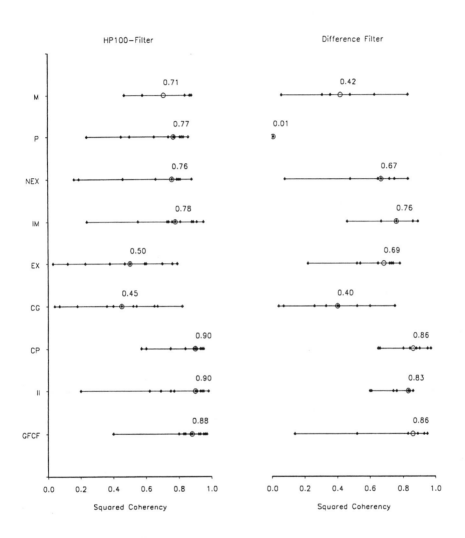

Fig. 4.9: OECD, Multivariate Results, Short Cycle, Maximum Squared
Coherency (*sc*)

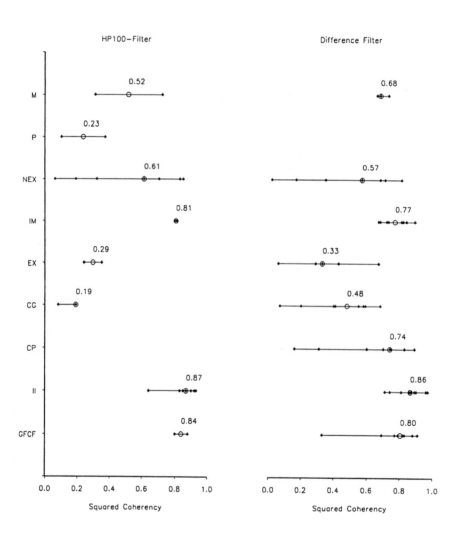

Fig. 4.10: OECD, Multivariate Results, Long Cycle, (Absolute) Phase Shift

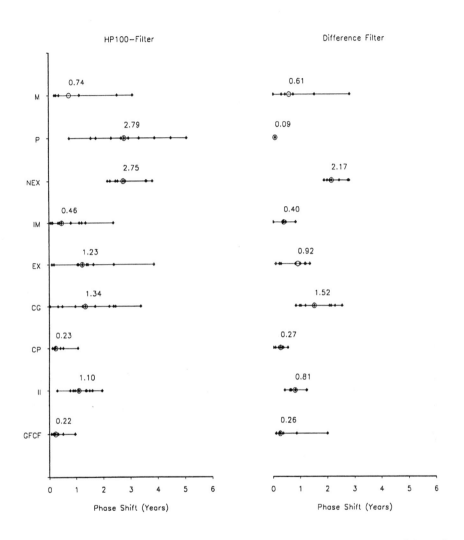

Fig. 4.11: OECD, Multivariate Results, Short Cycle, (Absolute) Phase Shift

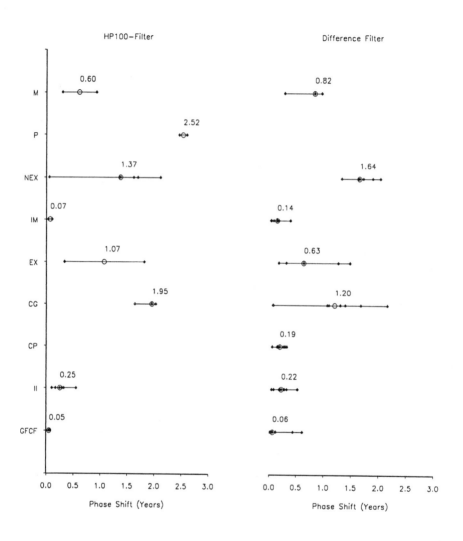

Fig. 4.12: OECD, Multivariate Results, Long Cycle, Gain

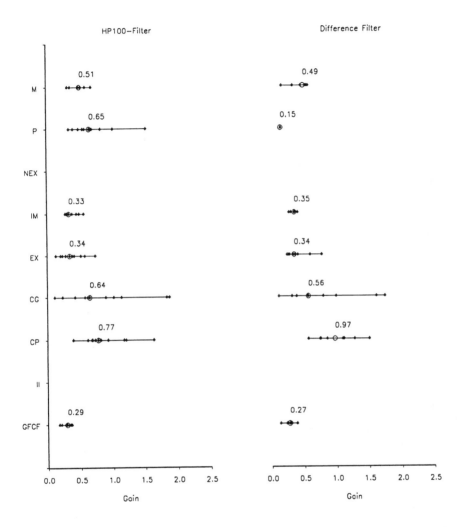

Fig. 4.13: OECD, Multivariate Results, Short Cycle, Gain

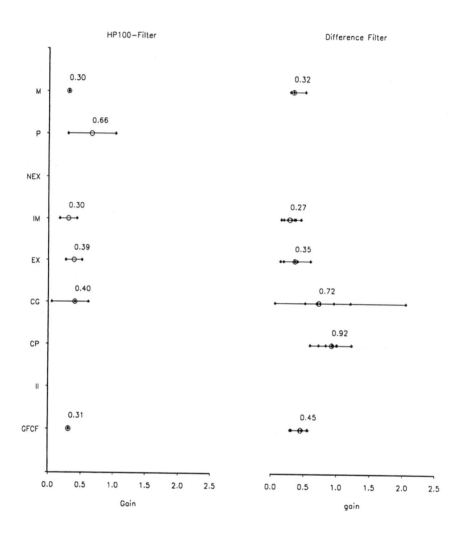

4.3   Prewar Period

In this section, business cycle stylized facts in the prewar period (1870-1914) are analyzed. The analysis follows the paper of Backus and Kehoe (1992) insofar as the same data set is used,[32] but for the description of the stylized facts ME spectral estimation is applied as in the previous chapter. This procedure enables us to compare the results with the stylized facts for the postwar period; moreover, it is possible to judge the robustness of the outcome by comparing them with the results in Backus and Kehoe (1992) obtained with time domain techinques, and to demonstrate again the superiority of spectral analysis for the description of business cycle stylized facts.

In the analysis of historical stylized facts and the comparison with postwar results one faces a serious problem: Postwar economic data are available from official statistics, although there quality is often questionable. For the prewar period, series like the GDP and its components were not gathered officially,[33] but have to be computed respectively estimated from available series. Therefore, one can hardly look upon the estimated series as being consistent with the postwar data; moreover, an international comparison is rather difficult. Given this situation, the results presented here must be interpreted very carefully, always bearing in mind that they might be specific for the estimates under analysis (see Borchardt (1976), p. 80-81).

One of the major topics in this research field is the question whether prewar output fluctuations are more volatile than in the postwar period, which is a widely accepted empirical regularity. Lucas (1977), does not include it to his list of stylized facts (see Chapter 1 of this study, p. 3). Nevertheless, he (p. 218) describes "[...] *the general reduction in amplitude of* all *series*

---

[32] I am very grateful to Prof. Backus for providing me with their data set.

[33] The *System of National Accounts* (SNA) as it is used today was developed in connection with the growing acceptance of Keynesian theory since the 1930s. First estimates for national income became available in 1993 (1928-38, 26 countries). The first version of the SNA was published in 1953. The system containing a set of international standard conventions was subjected to a number of major revisions (1968, 1993). In 1983, only about 55 per cent of the market economies computed their national accounts according to the latest version (see Beckstein (1987)).

in the twenty-five years following World War II" as "*[...] too striking a phe-nomenon to pass over without comment"*. But this view is subject to doubt. Backus and Kehoe (1992), pp. 865-866 report the discussion on the stylized fact for the US-case, for which it seems that the heavy fluctuations before World War I are at least partly due to measurement errors.[34] For Germany, this stylized fact is also questionable, as it is shown by Borchardt (1976).[35]

Besides the analysis of international output fluctuations, Backus and Ke-hoe (1992) examine the components of the national product and the fluc-tuations in prices and money stock. The (annual) series under analysis are Output (Y), Private Consumtion (CP), Investment (I), Governmental Con-sumtion (CG), Money Stock (M), Price Level (P), and Net Exports (NEX) [36] for the countries Australia (AUS), Denmark (DNK), Germany (GER), Italy (ITA), Japan (JPN), Norway (NOR), Sweden (SWE), United Kingdom (GBR), and United States (USA) in the period 1870-1986. France is not included in their data set. To judge the change over time in the characteris-tics of this very long series and to take into account the two sever structural breaks caused by the two world wars, the observation period is devided in the prewar period (1870-1914), the interwar period (1929-1939), and the postwar period (1950-1986).

Backus and Kehoe (1992) use time domain techniques to determine the stylized facts, as it was done at the beginning of Chapter 2 for the German postwar GDP. Before it is possible to compute the sample moments, they have to make their series stationary. This is done throughout their paper by

---

[34] See Romer (1986), Romer (1989), and Balke and Gordon (1989).

[35] In Borchardt (1976), the question is analyzed whether it is justified for the German economy to look upon *Wachstumszyklen* (cyclical growth) as typical for the postwar business cycle, while the *klassischer Konjunkturzyklus* (classical business cycle) is the typical prewar business cycle pattern. The former is characterized by growth rates fluctuating with positive sign, i.e. the growth process alternates between acceleration and deceleration. In the latter case, the variable under consideration actually declines in a recession, i.e. the lower turning point of the growth rates is negative (see Borchardt (1976), p. 74, Figure 1). Borchardt (1976), p. 98 concludes that the assertion of smoother postwar fluctuations for Germany can only be maintained if the comparison is restricted to the interwar period.

[36] For the exact date sources see Backus and Kehoe (1992), Appendix A, pp. 883-885.

applying the HP100 filter to the data (in logs) without taking into account the possibility of a difference-stationary series.

The following list contains the main conclusions of Backus and Kehoe (1992):

1. Investment is about 2-4 times as variable as output.

2. Consumption is about as variable as output.

3. Investment and consumption are procyclical.

4. The trade balance is generally countercyclical.

5. Governmental consumption does not have a clear cyclical structure concerning the correlation with output.

6. In the prewar period, price levels fluctuate procyclical; in the postwar period, they fluctuate countercyclical.[37]

7. While the fluctuations in the interwar period are larger than in the postwar period, there is no consistent pattern in the comparison between the fluctuations before World War I and after World War II.

In the following, I apply ME-spectral estimation to the Backus/Kehoe-data set in the prewar period (1870-1914)[38] to show as in the previous part of the study that it is possible to be more specific concerning the stylized facts, and to judge whether the results in Sections 4.2.1 and 4.2.2 are typical for the postwar period. The interwar period has to be left out of analysis, because it is too short to identify cycles at business cycle frequencies.

A discussion of the data sources and the quality of the estimates, which is done in detail in Backus and Kehoe (1992), Section 1, pp. 866-870, would

---

[37] A comparable result for the United States and the United Kingdom can be found in Correia, Neves and Rebelo (1992).

[38] Australia: 1861-1914, Canada: 1870-1914, Denmark: 1870-1914, Germany: 1850-1913, Italy: 1861-1914, Japan: 1885-1914, Norway: 1865-1938, Sweden: 1861-1914, United Kingdom: 1870-1914, and United States: 1869-1914.

be beyond the scope of this section. But as stated above, the results for the cyclical structure might be dependent on the estimate under analysis. To give an impression of this problem, I compare the univariate spectra GNP-estimates for Canada of Urquhart (1986) (CANY1) and Altman (1992) (CANY2, CANY3) in the prewar period. The results are displayed in Figure 4.14 and Table 4.1. Figure 4.14 contains only the spectra for the HP100[39] filtered series.

Fig. 4.14:   Comparison of the Cyclical Structure of Canadian GNP-Estimates, 1870-1914

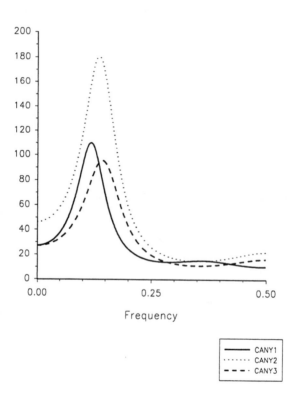

---

[39] HP100: Hodrick-Prescott filter with $\mu = 100$; see Appendix A.

Table 4.1: Canadian GNP-Estimates, Univariate Spectra

	Period	*pp*	Moduli	SNR
HP100				
CANY1	8.51	0.16	0.78	5.59
	2.78	0.07	0.52	
CANY2	7.39	0.18	0.76	6.11
CANY3	7.02	0.17	0.73	5.44
Diff.				
CANY1	5.83	0.08	0.51	4.01
CANY2	-	-	-	-
CANY3	-	-	-	-

[1]   Urquhardt (1986)
[2]   Adelman (1992), Version A
[3]   Adelman (1992), Version B

The difference between Urquhart's estimates of Canadian real GNP and the revisions of Altman are caused by the use of different price indices. These different price indices lead to differences in the real output level and in the growth rates (see Altman (1992), pp. 471-472). Besides these long-run effects, there is also an obvious change in the pattern of the short-run fluctuations, as it can be seen from Figure 4.14 and Table 4.1.

For the HP100 filtered series, the spectrum of the Urquhardt estimate (CANY1) exhibits a peak at a cycle length of about 9 years, with a *pp* of 0.16, which is significantly smaller than the result for the postwar period, where the corresponding *pp* is about 0.5 (see Table 4.4 on p. 95). The long cycles in the Altman estimates (CANY2, CANY3) are shorter (7 years) and about the same *pp* (0.18, 0.17). The short cycle can only be found in CANY1. The comparison with the results for the difference filtered series shows that the cyclical structure is not robust: Only in CANY1 a cycle can be found with a length of about 6 years and a *pp* of 0.08.

The outcome is a good example for the importance of the choice of the detrending procedure and the choice of the series to be analyzed. Dependent on

114 4. Business Cycle Stylized Facts in the OECD Countries

this decision, totally different results might be obtained. Therefore, I present
again the results for both detrending methods, and, in the univariate case, for
all series available. Besides the output and price series of Canada, this is the
case for the United States, where output and price level estimates by Balke
and Gordon (1986) (USAY1, USAP1), Romer (1989) (USAY2, USAP2), and
Balke and Gordon (1989) (USAY3, USAP3) are analyzed.

4.3.1 Univariate Results

As in the previous sections, the results for both filter methods are presented
using error-bar type plots, although it is not possible to inteprete them in
the same way. The reason is that there are remarkably differences in the
availability of data. For example, the money stock and the price level are
complete for every country, but private consumption is only available for
Japan, Norway, Sweden, United Kingdom, and United States. But this type
of plots is still useful to get a visual impression of the outcome.

For the interpretation of the results it is again important to bear in mind
that the filtered series (in logs) are to be looked upon as percentage deviations
from the HP100 trend, and, in the other case, as growth rates.[40] The univariate results are displayed in Figures 4.15 - 4.19 and in Tables B.17 - B.23,
p. 181 ff. The moduli are not plotted, since they contain essentially the same
information as pp, as we have seen for the postwar period in the previous
sections.[41] In the HP100-filtered series, the cyclical structure is dominated
by a long cycle[42] with a length of about 8 years and a pp of 0.15-0.30. As
in the postwar period, the long cycle in M is longer than in output, both for
the detrended series and the growth rates. The short cycle has a length of
3-4 years and pps up to 0.2. For the difference filtered series, the spectrum is

---

[40] With the exception of NEX, for which the results are again presented for the filtered series in levels.

[41] The results for the moduli are displayed in Tables B.21 and B.22 on p. 185 f. The correlation coefficient between moduli and pp at the long cycle is about 0.74 (HP100 filter).

[42] As in the previous sections, a long cycle is defined as a cycle with a length greater or equal to 5 years; a short cycle has a length less than 5 years.

shifted to the high frequencies, i.e. the short cycles. The *pps* are in general higher for the short cycles now.

SNR is in general lower for the difference filtered series than for the HP100 filtered series. The highest *SNR* in the HP100 filtered series can be found in M (median: 12.31). For the other series, the median varies between 6 and 9,[43] which is comparable to the results for the postwar period (see Figure 4.7).

Looking at the output and its components, we see that the cycles in CG have the highest *pp* for both filtering methods; moreover, the *SNR* is also relatively high for this series. The *pps* of the investment cycles are smaller for both the deviations of the trend and the growth rates, with the exception of the short cycle: Here, the median of the *pps* is highest for the difference filtered series. The *SNRs* of the investment series are close to the results for CG.

These results coincide with the findings in Backus and Kehoe (1992) and the outcome for the OECD countries in the previous section. The only exception is CG, for which the fluctuations in the prewar period are more regular and the cycles have higher *pps* than even for the investment series. The result is robust with respect to the detrending procedure, as a comparison between the outcome for the HP100 and the difference filtered CG shows.

---

[43] See Table B.23 on p. 187.

Fig. 4.15: Historical Time Series, Univariate Results, Cycle Lengths, Long Cycle

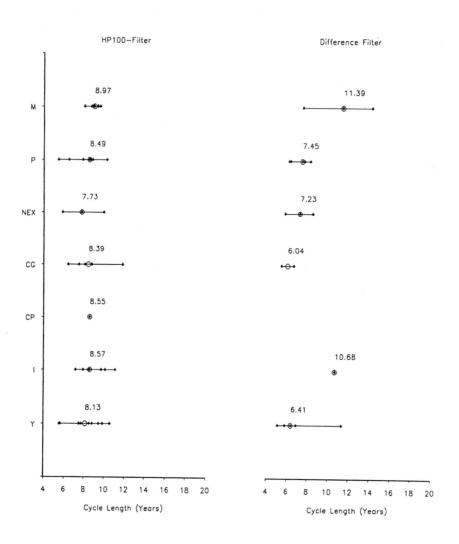

Fig. 4.16: Historical Time Series, Univariate Results, Cycle Lengths, Short Cycle

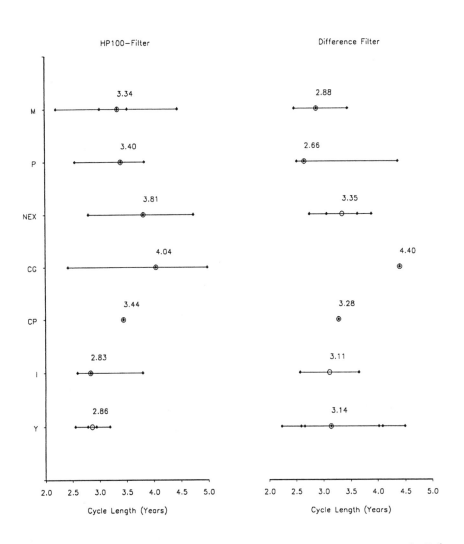

Fig. 4.17: Historical Time Series, Univariate Results, Peak Power, Long Cycle

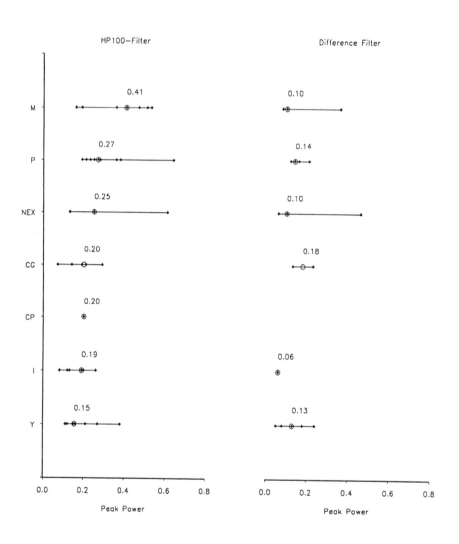

Fig. 4.18: Historical Time Series, Univariate Results, Peak Power, Short Cycle

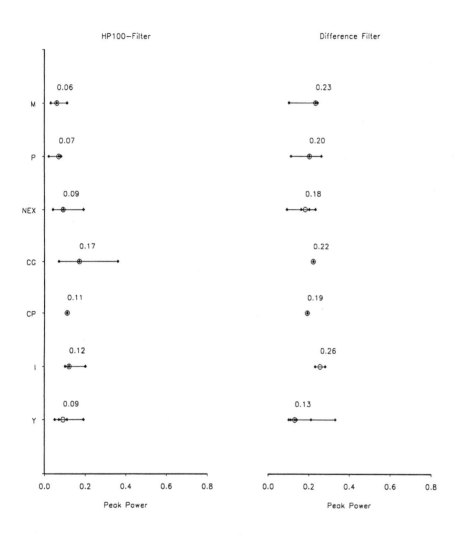

Fig. 4.19: Historical Time Series, Univariate Results, Signal-to-Noise Ratio (*SNR*)

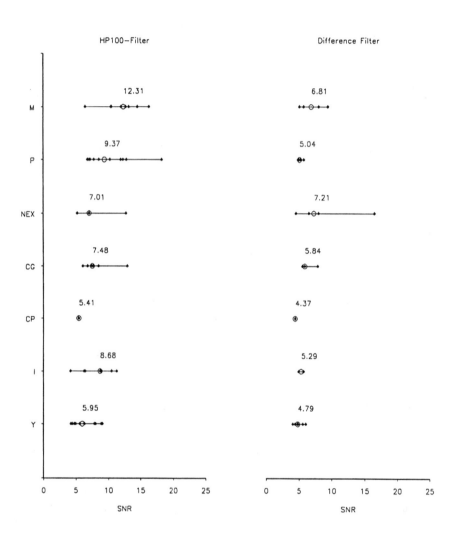

4.3.2   Multivariate Results

Figures 4.20 - 4.25 on p. 123 ff. contain the plots of the multivariate results. Detailed results can be found in Tables B.27 - B.32, p. 190 ff. For Canada and the United States, the output and price level estimates of Urquhart (1986) and Balke and Gordon (1986) are analyzed in the following, as it is done by Backus and Kehoe (1992).

Taken together, we see that the coherence between the output and the other series is smaller than in the postwar period. Between the cyclical structure in the investment series and the output series, there is a higher coherence at the long cycle than for the other output components. The median of sc is 0.72 for the HP100 filtered series and 0.66 for the difference filtered series.[44] The short cycle in output has only a small coherence with the short cycles in the investment series, both for the HP100 (0.23) and the difference filtered series (0.23).

Between the long output cycles and the respective cycles in CG and NEX, the coherence is smaller than for CP and the investment cycles.[45] The cyclical structure of the Y/CG-system exhibits very small scs; at the long cycle, they are smallest for both detrending methods. We have a median of 0.43, the result for the difference filtered system is 0.49. This coincides with the results for the postwar period (Figure 4.8 on p. 103).

Comparing it with the results for the other series under analysis, the relationship between output and M is relatively weak. Although M is available for all countries under analysis, multivariate cyclical structure could be detected only for CAN, DNK, JPN, and USA (Table B.27 and B.28 on p. 190 f.). This is similar to the small correlations between output and money stock reported in Backus and Kehoe (1992). Moreover, the result coincides with the findings for the postwar period in the previous sections.

Looking at the phase shift we see that the cycles in the investment series

---

[44] sc is higher for the HP100 filtered GDP/CP-system (3 results, see Table B.27 on p. 190).
[45] sc is higher for the difference filtered Y/NEX-system (2 results, see Table B.28 on p. 191).

are in phase with the output cycles, i.e. the median of the phase shift is less than 1 year for both cycle lenghts and both detrending methods. The same result is obtained for the Y/CP-system, where the medians are of about the same order of magnitude. The long cycles in CG lead the long cycles in output with a shift of about 2 years, but this result is hard to interprete given the small sc s. The long cycles in the Y/NEX-system show an average phase shift of 3-4 years, i.e. given the respective cycle lengths, we can conclude that NEX are countercyclical.

The interpretation of the phase shift between the output cycles and the cycles in M is not easy, since it is based on few results only. For the HP100 filtered prices, we have a median of 1.4 years at the long cycle, which is clearly smaller than the result in the postwar period, where the prices are countercyclical with a phase shift of about 3 years at the long cycle. This outcome corresponds to the results in Backus and Kehoe (1992).[46]

Taken together, the results for the historical data set coincide with the stylized facts of postwar business cycles. However, there are two exceptions: The procyclical behaviour of the prices and the univariate cyclical structure of CG. The result for CG is an example for the precise information spectral analysis is able to provide: We see that the importance of the cycles in CG is higher than for the other components, while the coherence with the respective output cycles is only low.

---

[46] See p. 111.

Fig. 4.20: Historical Time Series, Multivariate Results, Long Cycle, Maximum Squared Coherency (*sc*)

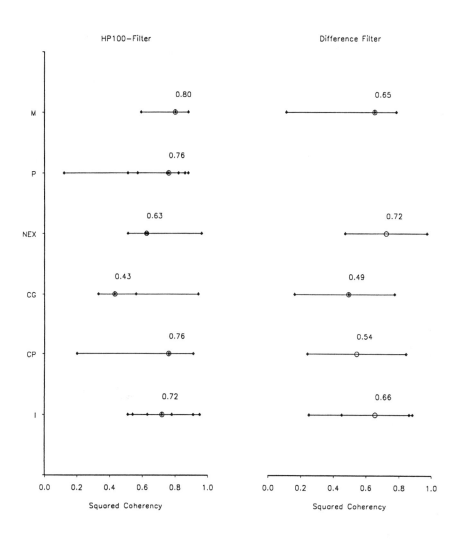

Fig. 4.21: Historical Time Series, Multivariate Results, Short Cycle, Maximum Squared Coherency (*sc*)

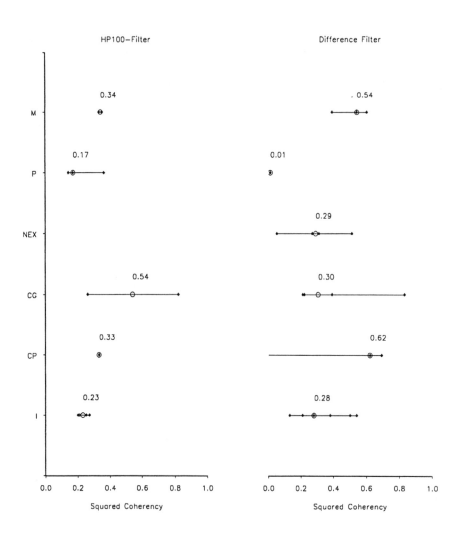

Fig. 4.22: Historical Time Series, Multivariate Results, Long Cycle, (Absolute) Phase Shift

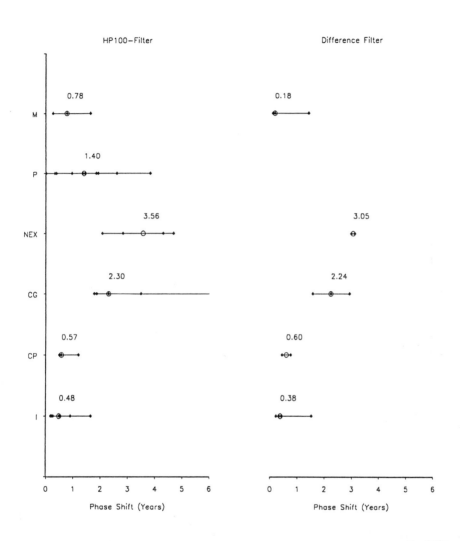

Fig. 4.23: Historical Time Series, Multivariate Results, Short Cycle, (Absolute) Phase Shift

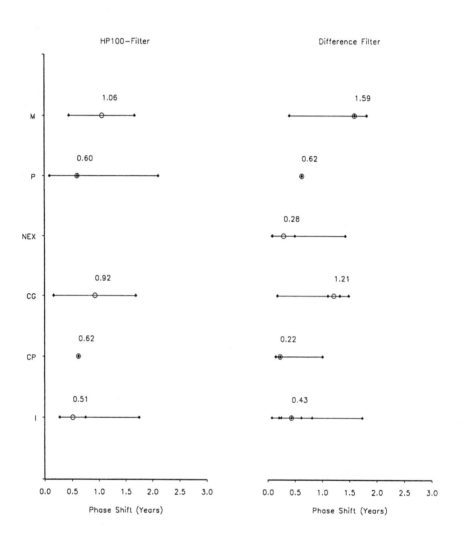

Fig. 4.24: Historical Time Series, Multivariate Results, Long Cycle, Gain

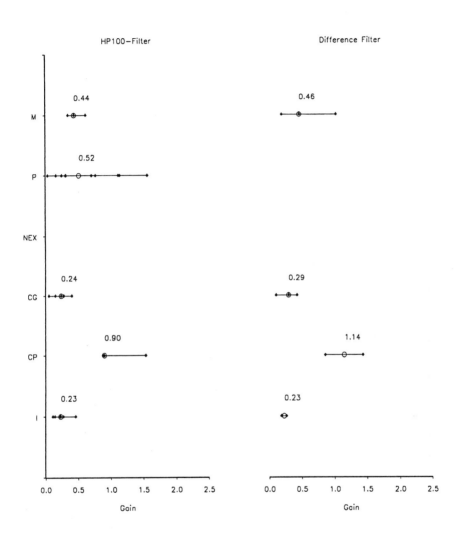

Fig. 4.25: Historical Time Series, Multivariate Results, Short Cycle, Gain

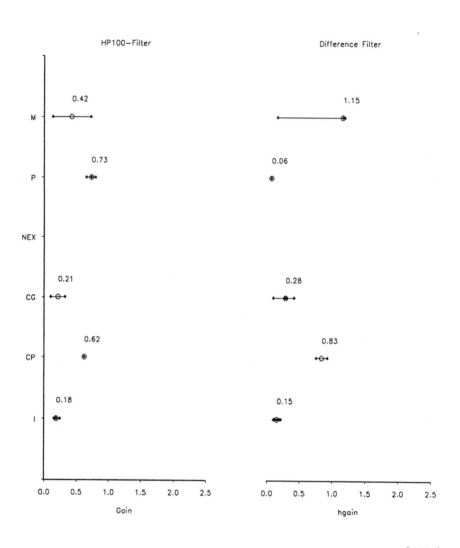

Chapter 5

Conclusion

The aim of this study was to describe business cycle stylized facts by applying novel spectral analysis methods. It was shown that Maximum Entropy spectral estimation is superior to the widely used time domain methods by providing far more detailed results. Moreover, this estimate is more suitable for the short macroeconomic time series than the normally used spectral estimate, the periodogram.

In Sections 4.2.1 and 4.2.2, the the stylized facts for 11 OECD countries in the postwar era were presented. To find out whether the business cycle pattern changes over time, the macroeconomic data set of Backus and Kehoe (1992) for the prewar era was examined in Section 4.3.1 and 4.3.2. As shown in Appendix A, we cannot distinguish reliably between trend and difference stationary series. Therefore, the outcome is presented for both the Hodrick-Prescott and the difference filter. This procedure enabled us to judge the robustness of the results with regard to the stationarity assumption.

Summing up the results from these sections, we have the following list of robust stylized facts:

> *SF1.* In aggregate output for both the prewar and the postwar period, a long and a short cycle can be found with lengths of 6-9 years and 3-4 years. For the postwar period, these cycles are concentrated in the investment series.

SF2. The long cycle is most prominent for the cyclical structure in fixed investment (but also appears in inventory investment), while the short cycle dominates the cyclical structure in inventory investment.

SF3. Comparing the output components in the postwar period, inventory investment is the series which is most strongly affected by the noise, while fixed investment exhibits the most regular fluctuations.

For the prewar period, there is some evidence that the fluctuations in CG are more regular than the investment fluctuations.

SF4. Between the long cycle in aggregate output and the long cycle in fixed investment, respectively between the short cycles in output and inventory investment, there is a strong coherence. This is also true for the cycles in private consumption and in the imports. For both the prewar and the postwar period, the weakest relationship can be found between the cycles in governmental consumption and the output cycles.

SF5. Between the output cycles and the cycles in the investment series, the phase shift is lowest, i.e. they are procyclical, which is also the case for imports and private consumption. For the postwar period, the exception is the long cycle in inventory investment, which lags the long output cycle with a phase shift of about 1 year.

SF6. For both the prewar and the postwar period, the coherence between the cycles in the monetary aggregates and the output cycles is only small.

SF7. In the postwar period, net exports and prices fluctuate countercyclically. In the prewar period, there is some evidence that the fluctuations in net exports are also countercyclical. This is not the case for the price cycles.

SF1, *SF2*, *SF4*, and *SF5* lead to the conclusion that the business cycle must be interpreted as investment cycle, for which the Second-Order Accelerator developed by C. Hillinger provides a convincing explanation. Another interesting result is the lead-lag structure between output cycles and cycles in the money stock and governmental consumption: Evidence for countercyclical fiscal or monetary policy could not be found (*SF4*, *SF6*). Price cycles are countercyclical in the postwar period (*SF7*), which is an important stylized fact with regard to Real Business Cycle theory. Net exports have a dampening effect on the business cycle (*SF7*).

Of course, there are unsolved problems left in this study. Given that the cyclical structure in macroeconomic time series has turned out not to be country specific, an extension of the analysis to the phenomenon of the international business cycle seems promising. Moreover, it is necessary to examine the robustness of the cyclical structure in more detail. But taken together, it was demonstrated that Maximum Entropy spectral analysis is an appropriate tool for describing business cycle stylized facts. Based on this method, the set of basic stylized facts of traditional business cycle theory could be convincingly confirmed and extended.

Appendix A

The Detrending Problem

A.1   Spurious Cycles

Although not the main topic of this study, the long-run characteristics of the GDPs of Australia (AUS), Canada (CAN), Denmark (DNK), France (FRA), (Western) Germany (GER), Italy (ITA), Japan (JPN), Norway (NOR), Sweden (SWE), United Kingdom (GBR), and United States (USA) are examined in the following sections.[1] I restrict the analysis to univariate time series; cointegration relationships are not examined here.

The reason is that to make use of the informations on business cycle stylized facts spectral analysis is able to provide, stationary time series are necessary. But a huge number of economic time series are non-stationary, and therefore, one has to remove this long-run component from the data. As it was said in Chapter 2, the long-run characteristics are important for the desription of the regularity in the short-run fluctuations, insofar as the structure might be seriously distorted if inappropriate detrending procedures are chosen.

Of course it would be optimal for this purpose if the trend-generating process was known. Two types of non-stationarity have been extensively discussed in the econometric literature: The difference stationary (DS-) model and the trend stationary (TS-) model. In equations (A.1) and (A.2), two simple examples for these models are given.

DS–model:

$$(1 - L)y_t = \zeta_t; \tag{A.1}$$
$$\zeta_t = \alpha_1\zeta_{t-1} + \alpha_2\zeta_{t-2} + \ldots + \alpha_p\zeta_{t-p} + u_t;$$

---

[1] Annual data at constant prices; the observation period is 1960-1991, with the exception of Germany, where it is 1960-1989 to avoid the structural break caused by the reunification. Data source: OECD Statistical Compendium, 1994.

TS-model:

$$y_t = a + bt + \zeta_t; \tag{A.2}$$
$$\zeta_t = \alpha_1 \zeta_{t-1} + \alpha_2 \zeta_{t-2} + \ldots + \alpha_p \zeta_{t-p} + u_t;$$

In both cases, the u_t are assumed to be white noise with variance σ^2 and mean 0. The first model is an ARIMA$(p, 1, 0)$ model, i.e. the non-stationarity is due to a unit root and can be removed by taking first differences. Model 2 is a linear time trend superimposed by a stationary AR(p)-process. In this case, the non-stationary part of the series can be removed by substracting the linear trend. As stated above, it would be optimal to know the exact nature of the non-stationarity of the series. But this is not the case in general, and therefore a method has to be found for deciding whether a series is DS or TS. Alternatively we have to apply a detrending procedure which is reasonably robust against misspecification of the trend-generating process.

Since we do not know the trend generating process in general, the danger of distorting the residual structure applying a wrongly chosen detrending method might arise. Inappropriate detrending may affect the structure of the residuals in two ways: A wrong detrending procedure may generate spurious cycles in cases where there is no cyclical structure in the residuals. Moreover, if applied in the wrong situation, a detrending procedure may distort existing cyclical structure.

The knowledge on the possibility of distorting the cyclical structure of a series by choosing an inappropriate detrending procedure is not new but well known among business cycle researches who are working empirically. For example, Mitchell (1927), pp 213-221 discusses the problem in detail. Concerning the influence of a moving-average-trend he writes (pp. 215-216):

> *In business-cycle work, moving averages will yield a satisfactory line of trend, if the trend is linear, if the period of the average corresponds to the duration of the cycles, and if the cycles are regular both in duration and intensity. These conditions are seldomly strictly satisfied. If the true trend is a convex curve, a*

> moving average lies above the curve, and so produces errors in
> the cyclical deviations, the magnitude of which increases with the
> convexity of the curve and the period of the moving average. If
> the true trend is concave, errors of opposite sign result.

A well known example for the possibility of generating spurious cyclical
structure in the residuals using an inappropriately chosen detrending procedure is the result of Granger (1966), who found that economic variables
exhibit a 'typical spectral shape', i.e. they have spectra which have most of
their power in the low-frequency range.[2] But this result may be due to his
detrending procedure: he uses an exponential linear trend, and this trend
function is known to generate a long wave in the residuals, if the growth
rates of the original data are not constant, or, respectively, are not fluctuating around a constant level. This long wave will lead to a spectrum which
has most of its power in the low-frequency range. This is a very illustra-
tive example, and therefore in Figure A.1 the periodograms of the detrended
GDPs (in levels) are displayed. The trend function is the linear exponential
time trend $\tilde{y}_t = a\, exp(bt)$ as in the paper of Granger (1966), which is fitted
to the data using nonlinear least squares.

We see that all series exhibit the 'typical spectral shape' found by Granger.
They all have peaks in the periodogram at a cycle length of about 32 years.
For all series, the variance of these long waves explains between 30 and 90
per cent of the series' variance.

These cycle lengths are clearly too long to be interpreted as business
cycles, beside of the fact that it does not make much sense to identify 30
years long cycles with a sample size of 32 years. How could this happen? As
stated above, the appropriate use of an exponential trend requires growth
rates which fluctuate around a constant level. It is well known that in indus-
trialized countries, the growth rates follow a negative trend since about 1960.

---

[2] A further example from the literature is the Kuznets-cycle which was already mentioned
in the introduction. This cycle can be generated by applying the data transformation
used by Kuznets (centered first differences of nonoverlapping 5-year moving averages) to
a series which does not have original cyclical structure (see Sargent (1979), pp. 249-251).

Of course, this is also true for the countries under analysis, and therefore, the result is not surprising. As it will be shown in this and the following sections, the question wether a detrending procedure is suitable or not cannot always be so easily answered as in the case of the exponential trend, where a look at the plot of the growth rates will be sufficient.

Fig. A.1: The 'Typical Spectral Shape'

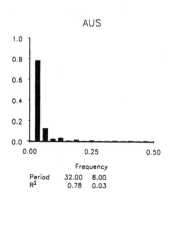

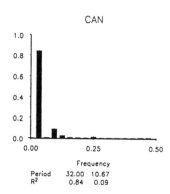

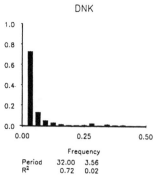

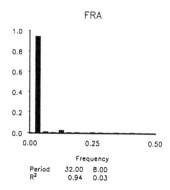

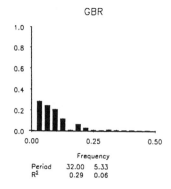

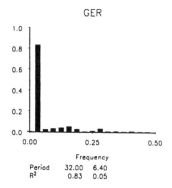

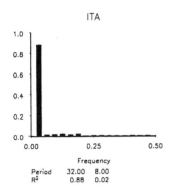

ITA

Period	32.00 8.00
R^2	0.88 0.02

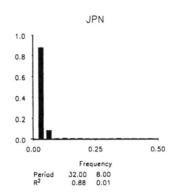

JPN

Period	32.00 8.00
R^2	0.88 0.01

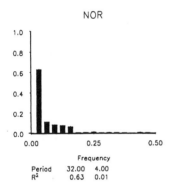

NOR

Period	32.00 4.00
R^2	0.63 0.01

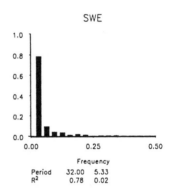

SWE

Period	32.00 5.33
R^2	0.78 0.02

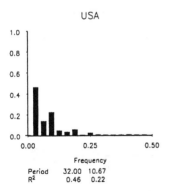

USA

Period	32.00 10.67
R^2	0.46 0.22

Following the influential papers of Chan, Hayya and Ord (1977) and Nelson and Plosser (1982), there is a body of literature analyzing the distorting effects of a wrongly chosen detrending procedure. In the following, the distortions caused by a difference filter if applied to a TS-model and the distortions caused by the Hodrick-Prescott filter if applied to a DS-model are compared in the frequency space using the *power transfer functions* of the respective filters.

The Hodrick-Prescott (HP-) filter, which was recently developed by Hodrick and Prescott (1980), is widely used[3] because of its flexibility and robustness against misspecifications (see Hillinger, Reiter and Woitek 1992b). Nevertheless, it has shown that this filter can cause distortions in the residual structure, too (see Harvey and Jaeger (1991) and King and Rebelo (1993)). To measure the influence of a filter on the cyclical structure of an input series, the power transfer function (*ptf*) is used. The HP-filter ($\phi(L)^{HP}$) can be derived from the minimization problem

$$\min_{\tilde{y}_t} \left(\sum_{t=1}^{T} (y_t - \tilde{y}_t)^2 + \mu \sum_{t=2}^{T-1} \{(\tilde{y}_{t+1} - \tilde{y}_t) - (\tilde{y}_t - \tilde{y}_{t-1})\}^2 \right) ; \tag{A.3}$$

where y_t is the input series of the filter, and the output series $\tilde{y}_t$ is chosen to minimize the above expression. The parameter μ determines the relative weight between the first term, which measures the goodness of fit, and the second term, which is a measure for the variation of the trend. For annual data, this parameter is usually set to 100.

Solving the minimization problem in equation (A.3) and using backshift-operator notation gives

$$\phi(L)_{I(0)}^{HP} = \frac{(1 - L)^2 (1 - L^{-1})^2}{\mu^{-1} + (1 - L)^2 (1 - L^{-1})^2}; \tag{A.4}$$

---

[3] For recent applications of the HP-filter see e.g. Baxter (1991), Backus and Kehoe (1992), Brandner and Neusser (1992), and Smeets (1992).

where the subscript 'I(0)' denotes that the input series of the filter is $I(0)$, i.e. integrated of order 0. If applied to an $I(1)$-series, i.e. a series which is stationary after first differences (integrated of order 1, DS), the filter becomes

$$\phi(L)_{I(1)}^{HP} = \frac{(1-L)(1-L^{-1})^2}{\mu^{-1} + (1-L)^2(1-L^{-1})^2};$$ (A.5)

Using this result to compute the *ptfs* of the HP-filter if applied to an I(0)-series, we get

$$|\phi(\omega)_{I(0)}^{HP}|^2 = \left(\frac{4(1-\cos(\omega))^2}{\mu^{-1} + 4(1-\cos(\omega))^2} \right)^2;$$ (A.6)

For the *ptf* of a HP-filter if applied to an $I(1)$-series we have

$$|\phi(\omega)_{I(1)}^{HP}|^2 = \frac{8(1-\cos(\omega))^3}{(\mu^{-1} + 4(1-\cos(\omega))^2)^2};$$ (A.7)

The *ptf* of a first order difference filter if applied to an $I(0)$-series is

$$|\phi(\omega)_{I(0)}^{1D}|^2 = 2(1-\cos(\omega));$$ (A.8)

The plots of the three *ptfs* in equations (A.6), (A.7), and (A.8) are given in Figure A.2.

If a difference filter is applied to a $I(0)$-series, the influence of cycles with frequencies less than 0.17 is reduced, i.e. the *ptf* takes values less than 1, while the influence of cycles with frequencies higher than 0.17 is amplified, i.e. the *ptf* takes values greater than 1. This frequency corresponds to a cycle length of about 6 years.

It can be seen that if a HP100-filter[4] is applied to a I(1)-series, $|\phi(L)_{I(1)}^{HP}|^2$ has a maximum at the frequency $\lambda = 0.07$. The corresponding period is

---

[4] Hodrick-Prescott filter with $\mu = 100$: HP100 filter.

about 14 years. If the HP100 filter is applied in the right case, i.e. if the series is I(0), the *ptf* shows that cycles with business cycle frequencies are left unchanged, while cyclical structure at smaller frequencies is more or less removed from the series.

The above considerations point out that applying a filter in the wrong situation causes severe distortions of the univarite cyclical structure. Harvey and Jaeger (1991) show that the relationship between series is also affected by using the HP-filter if it is not appropriate.

In the bivariate case, HP- detrended random walks might show high correlations between spurious cycles. Harvey and Jaeger (1991) demonstrate this by computing the asymptotic distribution of the sample cross correlations of two independent stationary series, which is given by (see Brockwell and Davis 1991, p. 410)

$$\rho_{jk}(\tau) \sim AN\left(0, T^{-1} \sum_{h=-\infty}^{\infty} \rho_{jj}(h)\rho_{kk}(h)\right);\qquad\text{(A.9)}$$

The spectra of the two HP(100)-filtered random walks can be computed by

$$f_i(\omega) = \frac{8\left(1 - cos(\omega)\right)^3}{\left(\frac{1}{\mu} + 4\left(1 - cos(\omega)\right)^2\right)^2}\,\sigma_i^2; \quad i = j, k;\qquad\text{(A.10)}$$

Taking the inverse Fourier transform of the spectra gives the autocovariances and the autocorrelations of the two series:

$$\gamma_{ii}(\tau) = \sigma_i^2 \int_{-\pi}^{\pi} \frac{cos(\omega\tau)8\left(1 - cos(\omega)\right)^3}{\left(\frac{1}{\mu} + 4\left(1 - cos(\omega)\right)^2\right)^2}\,d\omega;$$

$$\text{(A.11)}$$

$$\rho_{ii}(\tau) = \frac{\gamma_{ii}(\tau)}{\gamma_{ii}(0)}; \quad \tau = 1, \dots; \quad i = j, k;$$

With equation (A.9) it is now possible to compute the standard deviation for the cross correlations. Harvey and Jaeger (1991) set $\sigma_i^2 = 1$ and use the first 100 autocorrelations to approximate the infinite sum in equation (A.9). Doing this for our special problem (sample size $N = 30$; annual data, i.e. $\mu = 100$), one obtains for the cross correlations a standard deviation of 0.26. If one assumes a normal distribution, this means a probability of about 34 per cent of cross correlations exceeding 0.25 in absolute value.

Fig. A.2: Power Transfer Function (*ptf*) of the HP100- and the Difference Filter

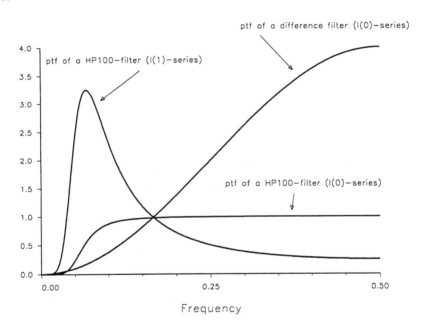

A.2   Persistence of Shocks

In this section, I will briefly discuss other implications of the choice between the DS– and the TS–model for business cycle modelling. If the DS–model is the true model, a separation between trend and fluctuations is not possible, and the effect of a shock cannot be transitory (as implied by the TS–model), but has to be permanent.

Until the the beginning of the 80s, the view of Hicks (1965), p. 4, was predominant, that at least for statistical purposes it is possible to separate between trend and fluctuations like in additive component models:

> *The distinction between trend and fluctuation is a statistical distinction; it is an unquestionably useful distinction for statistical summarizing. Since economic theory is to be applied to statistics, which are arranged in this manner, a corresponding arrangement of theory will (no doubt) often be convenient. But this gives us no reason to suppose that there is anything corresponding to it on the economic side which is at all fundamental. We have no right to conclude, from the mere existence of the statistical device, that the economic forces making for trend and for fluctuation are any different, so that they have to be analyzed in different ways. It is inadvisable to start our economics from the statistical distinction, though it will have to come in at an appropriate point, as an instrument of application.*

Based on the Dickey–Fuller test, a widely used method to decide between the DS- and the TS-model, the more recent research finds that for a great number of economic time series, the hypothesis of a unit root cannot be rejected, and therefore, that a DS–model represents the non-stationarity better than a TS–model. This means that even for *"statistical summarizing"*, the application of additive component models to separate fluctuations from growth is not advisable for two reasons: the distortion of cyclical structure and the different implications concerning the persistence of shocks.

These results have been very influential for economic theory. For example, the inability of rejecting the unit-root hypothesis excluded monetary shocks, which are looked upon as having only transitory influence (see e.g. Nelson and Plosser 1982, p. 159), as source for business fluctuations, and therefore was one of the reasons of the early popularity of Real-Business-Cycle models (see Rudebusch 1992, p. 662). Section A.3 critically reconsiders the evidence in favour of unit roots.

In the context discussed here, the main problem of the choice between the DS– and the TS–model is not the question whether shocks have a permanent influence or not. For the description of the cyclical characteristics of business cycles it is more important not to distort the cyclical structure by the choice of the wrong model (see Section A.1). But nevertheless, the persistence of shocks is an interesting point, and therefore, a short discussion is given in this section based on the procedure in Rudebusch (1992) and (1993), who analyzes the different implications for the duration of shocks for postwar quarterly U.S. macroeconomic data. In the following, his procedure is applied to the GDP-data.[5]

First, simple versions of the TS- and the DS-model are fitted to the data using OLS [6]. The TS-model is

$$y_t = \alpha + \beta t + \rho_1 y_{t-1} + \rho_2 y_{t-2} + u_t; \qquad (A.12)$$

and for the DS-model, which is estimated in first differences, we have

$$(1 - L)y_t = \alpha + \rho(1 - L)y_{t-1} + u_t; \qquad (A.13)$$

The parameter estimates are displayed in Table A.1 and Table A.2. As additional information, the tables contain also R^2_{adj} and the portmanteau test statistic $Q^\star$ (see Ljung and Box (1978)). The null hypothesis of this test is "H_0: *The residuals are white noise*", which is rejected if the residuals are significantly autocorrelated. The test statistic $Q^\star$ follows a χ^2-distribution, The number in brackets under $Q^\star$ denotes the probability of a higher value. From the $Q^\star$-statistic we see that the white-noise hypothesis for the residuals can only be rejected if one allows for error probabilities of more than 10 per

---

[5] The data are transformed by taking logarithms. The observation period is 1960-1991, with the exception of Germany, where it is 1960-1089 in order to avoid problems with the structural break caused by reunification. Data Source: OECD Statistical Compendium, 1994.

[6] In order to avoid additional difficulties with the choice of a model selection criterion, a second order AR-model is automatically chosen.

cent. Based on the results in the tables, both models appear to be plausible for our data set.

Table A.1: TS-Model

	$\hat{\alpha}$	$\hat{\beta}$	$\hat{\rho}_1$	$\hat{\rho}_2$	$\hat{\sigma}_u$	R^2	$Q^\star$
AUS	1.683	0.004	0.870	−0.008	0.019	0.997	6.209
	(0.877)	(0.003)	(0.177)	(0.175)			(0.797)
CAN	0.725	0.001	1.078	−0.133	0.021	0.997	9.552
	(0.981)	(0.003)	(0.199)	(0.204)			(0.481)
DNK	2.257	0.004	0.760	0.060	0.021	0.994	9.125
	(1.093)	(0.002)	(0.196)	(0.180)			(0.520)
FRA	1.068	0.001	1.148	−0.221	0.012	0.999	3.210
	(0.525)	(0.001)	(0.188)	(0.178)			(0.976)
GBR	4.204	0.007	1.117	−0.459	0.019	0.993	6.358
	(1.465)	(0.003)	(0.188)	(0.184)			(0.784)
GER	1.878	0.003	1.077	−0.211	0.020	0.994	14.042
	(1.041)	(0.002)	(0.200)	(0.194)			(0.171)
ITA	1.302	0.002	0.941	−0.039	0.021	0.997	8.531
	(0.941)	(0.003)	(0.197)	(0.186)			(0.577)
JPN	0.825	0.002	1.252	−0.319	0.023	0.998	14.745
	(0.433)	(0.002)	(0.185)	(0.174)			(0.142)
NOR	0.328	0.005	1.262	−0.286	0.017	0.998	7.748
	(1.361)	(0.002)	(0.188)	(0.223)			(0.653)
SWE	1.425	0.002	1.122	−0.228	0.015	0.996	8.677
	(0.833)	(0.002)	(0.209)	(0.190)			(0.501)
USA	4.657	0.008	1.004	−0.323	0.019	0.995	8.397
	(1.542)	(0.003)	(0.184)	(0.172)			(0.590)

To see that the DS- and the TS-model exhibit different economic behaviour we now turn to the cumulative responses of the respective models to a unit shock. These impulse responses can be computed from the MA-representations of the models. The infinite MA-process is defined as

$$y_t = \sum_{j=0}^{\infty} c_j u_{t-j}; \quad u_t \sim NID(0, \sigma^2);$$

If an AR-process is stationary, it has an infinite MA-representation like in the above equation (see e.g Brockwell and Davis 1991, p. 79 ff). The MA-

Table **A.2**: DS-Model

	$\hat{\alpha}$	$\hat{\rho}$	$\hat{\sigma}_u$	R^2	$Q^\star$
AUS	0.032	0.164	0.023	0.996	4.134
	(0.008)	(0.190)			(0.941)
CAN	0.024	0.371	0.024	0.996	6.131
	(0.009)	(0.197)			(0.804)
DNK	0.024	0.111	0.024	0.992	4.597
	(0.007)	(0.183)			(0.916)
FRA	0.012	0.633	0.015	0.998	3.415
	(0.006)	(0.150)			(0.970)
GBR	0.015	0.317	0.021	0.991	9.616
	(0.006)	(0.197)			(0.475)
GER	0.020	0.310	0.021	0.994	11.824
	(0.007)	(0.185)			(0.297)
ITA	0.027	0.238	0.022	0.996	7.150
	(0.008)	(0.176)			(0.711)
JPN	0.021	0.617	0.025	0.998	14.404
	(0.010)	(0.139)			(0.155)
NOR	0.021	0.390	0.017	0.998	7.175
	(0.007)	(0.172)			(0.709)
SWE	0.011	0.532	0.017	0.995	5.812
	(0.006)	(0.174)			(0.504)
USA	0.020	0.308	0.023	0.993	5.053
	(0.007)	(0.191)			(0.888)

parameter c_j measures the influence of a shock in period $t - j$ on y_t, the realisation of the AR-process in period t.

In a first step, the MA-representation of the DS-model in equation (A.13) is computed [7].

$$(1 - L)y_t = \rho(1 - L)y_{t-1} + u_t; \qquad \text{(A.14)}$$
$$(1 - (1 + \rho)L + \rho L^2)y_t = u_t;$$

Now both sides of the above equation are multiplied with $\sum_{j=0}^{\infty} c_j L^j$, which

---

[7] The constant term α is omitted because it has no influence on the impulse responses of the model.

results in

$$\sum_{j=0}^{\infty} c_j L^j (1 - (1+\rho)L + \rho L^2) y_t = u_t;$$

This equation can now be solved for the MA-parameters c_j. We get

$$c_j = (1+\rho)c_{j-1} - \rho c_{j-2}; \quad c_0 \ = \ 1;$$
$$c_{-1} \ = \ c_{-2} = 0; \qquad (A.15)$$

Solving this second order difference equation, one obtains the parameters of the MA-representation of the DS-model.

The same procedure can be applied to the TS-model. After taking differences and omitting the constant term, we get the following equation for the parameters of the MA-representation:

$$c_j = \rho_1 c_{j-1} + \rho_2 c_{j-2}; \quad c_0 \ = \ 1;$$
$$c_{-1} \ = \ c_{-2} = 0; \qquad (A.16)$$

Figure A.3 on the facing page gives a visual impression of the difference betweeen the two models.

It can be seen that for the DS-model, the unit shock increases, while for the TS-model, the unit shock dies very fast out to zero. An exception is the TS-model for the GDP of Norway, where the decrease of the influence of the shock is slower than for the other countries: After 30 years, there are still about 50 per cent of the shock present in the data.

These results show very clearly that the persistence of shocks is crucially dependent on the chosen type of non-stationarity. Besides the problem of spurious cyclicity, this is an additional reason why it is of great importance to have a method which is capable to decide reliably between the two models.

Fig. A.3: Impulse-Responses for the TS- and DS-Models

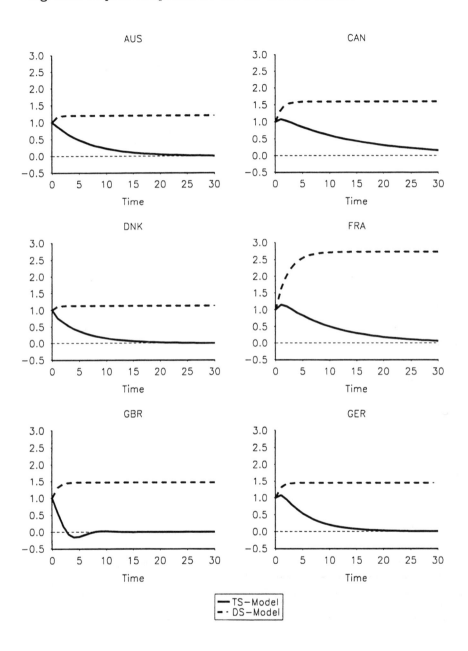

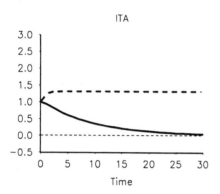

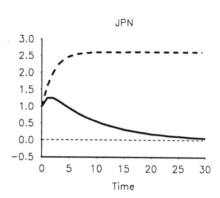

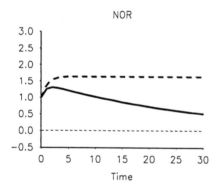

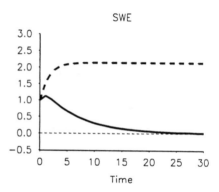

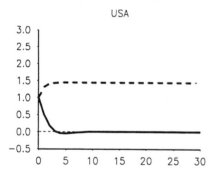

A.3   Testing for Unit Roots

A.3.1   The Dickey-Fuller Test

A widely used method for deciding whether a series is DS or not was developed by Dickey and Fuller (see Dickey 1976, Fuller 1976 p. 366-382, and Dickey and Fuller 1979). In its easiest form (random-walk model), one has to estimate the equation

$$y_t = \rho_1 y_{t-1} + u_t;$$

assuming that $u_t \sim NID(0, \sigma^2)$, and test the hypothesis $H_0 : \rho_1 = 1$ against the alternative $H_1 : |\rho_1| < 1$ computing the respective sample t-statistic. This statistic does not follow the usual t-distribution, but it is skewed towards negative values.

Other possibilites for testing the unit root-hypothesis are the likelihood-ratio test (Dickey and Fuller 1981) or the non-parametric test developed by Phillips (1987) and Phillips and Perron (1988).[8] For further analysis, I decided to use the Dickey-Fuller t-test, because the results for the other testing strategies are similar (see Rudebusch 1992).

If we want to use the Dickey-Fuller t-test to decide whether the TS- or the DS-model is the 'true' model, we have to estimate the augmented Dickey-Fuller equation[9]

$$y_t = \beta + \delta t + \rho_1 y_{t-1} + \alpha_2 (1 - L) y_{t-1} + u_t; \qquad (A.17)$$

and compute the test statistic $\hat{\tau}_s = (\hat{\rho}_1 - 1)/\hat{\sigma}_{\hat{\rho}_1}$. The problem is not whether the series in fact contains a linear trend, since the TS- as well as the DS-model allow for it, but whether the 'residuals' of this trend are DS or not (see Dickey, Bell and Miller 1986, p. 14).

Applying this test to the GDPs one obtains the following results:

---

[8] An overview of unit-root testing strategies is given by Perron (1988), pp.308-309.

[9] Again, the AR-order is fixed to 2 to avoid model selection problems and to make the results of Section A.2 comparable with those of Section A.3.2.

Table A.3: G7-Countries, Dickey-Fuller Test Statistics (t-Test) for the GDPs

	$\hat{\tau}_s$
AUS	-1.85
CAN	-0.68
DNK	-2.02
FRA	-1.96
GBR	-2.85
GER	-1.77
ITA	-1.33
JPN	-1.78
NOR	-0.21
SWE	-1.67
USA	-3.00

Critical values for the sample sizes of $N = 32$ and, for Germany, of $N = 30$ are not given by Dickey and Fuller, but in Table 8.5.2 of Fuller (1976), p. 373 one finds at the significance level 0.05 for a sample size of $N = 25$ a critical value of -3.60 and for a sample size of $N = 30$ a critical value of -3.50. Comparing these values with the test-statistics in the above table, we see that for each of the series, the null hypothesis $\rho_1 = 1$ could not be rejected at a 10 per cent significance level: In order to avoid distortions of the cyclical structure of the series and wrong implications concerning the persistence of shocks, it seems that it would be preferable to make the series stationary assuming a DS-model rather than a TS-model.

A.3.2   Limitations of the Dickey-Fuller Test

It is a well known fact that common unit-root tests have only low power against alternatives which are very similar to the unit-root model, i.e. the probability of rejecting the null hypothesis of a unit-root if it is not true is not very high (see e.g. Kwiatkowsky, Phillips and Schmidt 1991). 'Similar to the unit-root model' means that the AR-part of the TS-model has roots which are smaller than but close to unity, which is the case for a great number of macroeconomic time series (see e.g. West 1988, p. 202). Even Nelson and Plosser (1982) admit in their paper, where they found that for most of the US macroeconomic time series the unit root hypothesis could not be rejected: *"We recognize that none of the tests presented, formal and informal, can have power against a TS alternative with an AR root arbitrarily close to unity."* (p. 152).

But, as they argue, this is not an important point, because a TS–model with a root very close to unity would not exhibit characteristics which can be distinguished from those of a DS–model; otherwise, it should be possible to decide between the two models. In other words, the small power of the Dickey-Fuller test against alternatives which are too similar to the null model is not very interesting from an economic point of view, since the interpretation of the two models does not lead to clearly different results.

Rudebusch (1992, 1993) shows in a Monte-Carlo-Study that even if the two models exhibit totally different behaviour concerning the persistence of shocks, the DF-test is not capable of reliably distinguishing between them. To demonstrate this, he first fits plausible versions of the TS– and the DS–model to the same data set used by Nelson and Plosser (1982), and examines their characteristics concerning the duration of shocks. As we have seen for our data set in the previous section, the two models exhibit a totally different behaviour, and therefore, it should be expected based on the statement of Nelson and Plosser (1982) that the DF-test has enough power to reliably distinguish between the two alternatives.

In the following, I replicate the results of Rudebusch applying his procedure to the GDPs of AUS, CAN, DNK, FRA, GER, GBR, ITA, JPN, NOR, SWE, and USA as example data set. The TS- and the DS-model are simulated using the parameters from Tables A.1 and A.2:

TS-Model:

$$y_t = \alpha + \beta t + \rho_1 y_{t-1} + \rho_2 y_{t-2} + u_t; \ u_t \sim NID(0, \sigma_u^2);$$

DS-Model:

$$(1 - L)y_t = \alpha + \rho(1 - L)y_{t-1} + u_t; \ u_t \sim NID(0, \sigma_u^2);$$

For each model and each country, 10 000 samples were generated and $\hat{\tau}$, the augmented Dickey-Fuller test statistic was computed (see Section A.3.1). The results are empirical distributions of $\hat{\tau}$, conditional either on the DS–(denoted by $f(\hat{\tau}|DS)$) or on the TS–model (denoted by $f(\hat{\tau}|TS)$).

The easiest way to understand these results is to look at Figure A.4, where the estimates of the empirical distributions $f(\hat{\tau}|TS)$ and $f(\hat{\tau}|DS)$[10] for the US GDP are plotted.

---

[10] The estimates of the empirical distributions are carried through using a kernel density estimator (quartic kernel, see e.g. Härdle 1991). I am indebted to Markus Heintel for providing me with the estimation program.

Fig. A.4: Empirical Distributions of $\tau_s|DS$ and $\tau_s|TS$ for the US-GDP

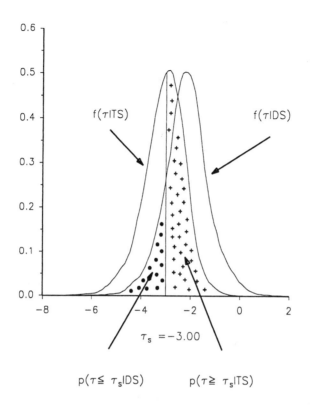

$\hat{\tau}_s$ is the augmented Dickey-Fuller test statistic for the US-GDP from Table A.3. The area under $f(\tau|DS)$ on the left side of $\hat{\tau}_s = -3.00$ represents the probability of a $\hat{\tau}$-value smaller than or equal to the test-statistic $\hat{\tau}_s$, if the DS-model is the true model $(p(\hat{\tau} \leq \hat{\tau}_s|DS))$. For the US-GDP, this probability is about 15 per cent (see Table A.4).

The area under $f(\tau|TS)$ on the right side of $\hat{\tau}_s = -3.00$ is the probability of a $\hat{\tau}$-value greater than or equal to $\hat{\tau}_s$, if the TS-model is the true model $(p(\hat{\tau} \geq \hat{\tau}_s|TS)$. For the US-GDP, this probability is 50 per cent. Obviously, it is not possible to decide clearly between the two models for the US-GDP. For the other countries, the results can be found in Table A.4.

Table A.4: $\hat{\tau}_s$ and the p-values of the DS- and the TS-models

	TS-Model	DS-Model
AUS	0.24	0.66
CAN	0.04	0.95
DNK	0.30	0.57
FRA	0.35	0.62
GBR	0.28	0.21
GER	0.18	0.70
ITA	0.11	0.85
JPN	0.26	0.68
NOR	0.02	0.98
SWE	0.18	0.73
USA	0.50	0.15

With the exception of Canada and Denmark, the outcome is similar to the results for USA. Summarizing the results of this section, it can be said that for the GDPs, the DF-test is not able to make a clear decision between the DS- and the TS-model. Since the two models do not show similar behaviour, this is a disturbing outcome.

A.3.3   Structural Breaks

If one allows for real world phenomena like strucutral breaks in the TS-model, the possibility of identifying a spurious unit root increases. Perron (1989) shows that if there is a structural break in the trend generating process, the standard Dickey-Fuller test is severly biased in favour of the unit root hypothesis. As examples, he uses the crash of 1929 and the oil price shock of 1973 and analyzes on the basis of US macroeconomic data the influence of two types of structural breaks on the ability of the Dickey-Fuller test to decide between a DS- and a TS-model. He distinguishes three types of structural breaks:

Model (A): Crash model

$$y_t = \mu + \beta t + \theta DU_t + \zeta_t; \quad t = 1, \ldots, t_b, \ldots, N; \qquad \text{(A.18)}$$

Model (B): Changing growth model

$$y_t = \mu + \beta t + \gamma D1T_t + \zeta_t; \quad t = 1, \ldots, t_b, \ldots, N; \qquad \text{(A.19)}$$

Model (C): Crash / Changing growth model

$$y_t = \mu + \beta t + \theta DU_t + \gamma D2T_t + \zeta_t; \quad t = 1, \ldots, t_b, \ldots, N; \qquad \text{(A.20)}$$

with

$$DU_t = \begin{cases} 1 & \text{if } t > t_b \\ 0 & \text{if } t \leq t_b \end{cases}$$

$$D1T_t = \begin{cases} t - t_b & \text{if } t > t_b \\ 0 & \text{if } t \leq t_b \end{cases}$$

$$D2T_t = \begin{cases} t & \text{if } t > t_b \\ 0 & \text{if } t \leq t_b \end{cases}$$

where t_b denotes the time of break and $\{\zeta_t\}$ is an arbitrary stationary stochastic process. For Model (A), the structural break influences only the level but not the slope of the long-run component, while for Model (B), only the slope of the trend is affected. Using Model (C), it is possible to have both types of shocks.

Assuming that $\{\zeta_t\}$ is white noise, Perron shows in a simulation study where he generates 10000 replications of each of the two models in equations (A.18) and (A.19) and fits a model of the form $y_t = \mu + \beta t + \alpha y_{t-1} + u_t$ to the simulated data, that as the influence of the exogenous shock increases, both in the case of Model (A) and of Model (B) the estimated parameter $\hat{\alpha}$ becomes more and more concentrated at a value close to unity. Therefore, the danger of identifying a spurious unit root in the case of a structural break in the trend generating process seems not to be negligible.

Perron offers a solution for this problem by extending the Dickey-Fuller test to make it possible to test the unit-root hypothesis against the alternative of a deterministic trend with structural break. In Tables IV.A to VI.B, pp. 1376-1377 of his paper one finds the critcal values of this extended test dependent on the significance level and λ, the ratio of the time of break to the total sample size.

Before we can apply Perron's test to the GDPs, we have first to ascertain that there is actually a structural break in the data. To do this, the procedure proposed in Greene (1993), p. 218, is applied. The first step is to get a visual impression of the time when the structural break occurs. For the GDPs, it is reasonable to assume the two oil price shocks 1974/75 and 1978/81 as possible candidates for the time of break. A formal test to find out the time of break is given by plotting the cumulative sum of recursive residuals (CUSUM) and the cumulative sum of squared residuals (CUSUMSQ) (see Brown, Durbin and Evans (1975)).

In the next step, we decide whether there is a structural break in the series at all using the test statistic after Harvey and Collier (1977) (HC); and finally, the Chow-test (see e.g. Greene (1993), p. 211-214) is performed to test whether we can reject the hypothesis that there is a change in the slope and the level of the trend at the time of break detected by the CUSUM- and CUSUMSQ-test.

To demonstrate the use of the CUSUM- and CUSUMSQ-test, the plots of these tests are displayed in Figure A.5 on p. 160 with the GDP of Denmark as example data set. For the other countries, the results are given in Table A.5.

Both the CUSUM- and the CUSUMSQ-plots show a structural break in the model. After the first oil price shock in 1973/74, the recursive residuals have the same sign until about 1984, crossing the border of the confidence interval at a 5 per cent significance level. CUSUMSQ also leaves the confidence intervall (5 per cent significance level) at 1975. After 1975, there is no tendency to return to the diagonal until 1982/83.

Table A.5: Testing for Structural Breaks in the GDPs

	Harvey-Collier	Chow	t_B	λ
AUS	0.47			
	(0.32)			
CAN	1.68	4.38	16	0.53
	(0.05)	(0.03)		
DNK	2.23	2.21	16	0.43
	(0.02)	(0.10)		
FRA	0.14			
	(0.44)			
GBR	2.36	4.45	13	0.43
	(0.01)	(0.02)		
GER	2.00	4.61	15	0.50
	(0.03)	(0.02)		
ITA	2.23	6.89	12	0.40
	(0.02)	(0.00)		
JPN	0.57			
	(0.29)			
NOR	2.38	6.39	16	0.53
	(0.01)	(0.01)		
SWE	2.37	1.66	22	
	(0.01)	(0.21)		
USA	1.49	4.10	12	0.40
	(0.07)	(0.03)		

p-values are given in brackets.

Fig. A.5: Denmark, GDP, CUSUM- and CUSUMSQ-Test

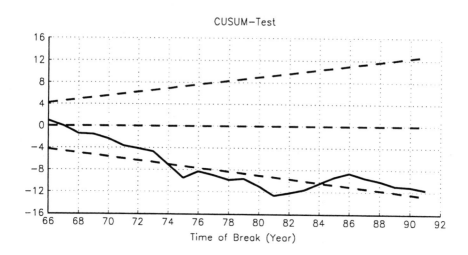

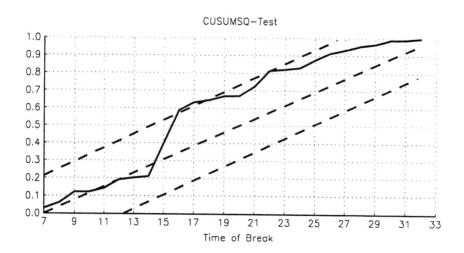

Table A.5 contains the results of the Harvey-Collier test, the Chow-test, the time of break (t_b) detected by CUSUM and CUSUMSQ, and λ, the ratio of the time of break to the sample size. We see that for Australia, France, and Japan, the Harvey-Collier test does not reject the hypothesis of a stable trend. Following this test one would assume a structural break for Sweden, but the Chow-test rejects the hypothesis that the level and slope of the trend change at the time of break detected by CUSUM and CUSUMSQ. For these countries, the procedure stops here. In the case of the other countries the visual impression of the CUSUM- and CUSUMSQ-plots as well as the results from the Harvey-Collier- and the Chow-test indicate that the hypothesis of a structural break cannot be rejected.

The results of the Perron-test are displayed in Table A.6. In all cases, the mixed-type model (C) was chosen, which allows for a structural break in both level and slope of the trend.

Table A.6: Perron-Test for the GDPs[1]

	λ	μ	β	θ	γ	τ_P	R^2_{adj}	Q^*
CAN	0.53	8.01	0.03	0.22	−0.01	-3.29	0.97	8.31
		(2.41)	(0.01)	(0.07)	(0.00)			(0.60)
DNK	0.53	4.93	0.01	0.07	−0.01	-1.58	0.99	6.97
		(3.08)	(0.01)	(0.06)	(0.01)			(0.73)
GBR	0.43	5.64	0.01	0.03	−0.00	-3.33	0.99	8.41
		(1.68)	(0.00)	(0.02)	(0.00)			(0.59)
GER	0.54	11.32	0.03	0.23	−0.02	-3.84	0.99	14.16
		(2.94)	(0.01)	(0.07)	(0.01)			(0.17)
ITA	0.40	6.60	0.03	0.14	−0.01	-3.06	0.97	8.30
		(2.14)	(0.01)	(0.05)	(0.00)			(0.60)
NOR	0.53	4.27	0.01	0.10	−0.01	-2.47	0.96	6.74
		(1.71)	(0.01)	(0.03)	(0.00)			(0.75)
USA	0.40	9.77	0.03	0.08	−0.01	-3.67	0.99	7.50
		(2.65)	(0.01)	(0.03)	(0.00)			(0.68)

[1]   Standard errors appear in parentheses.

The critical values for $\lambda = 0.4$ and $\lambda = 0.5$ can be found in Perron (1989), p. 1377, Table VI.B. For a significance level of 0.5 and 0.1, the test rejects the hypothesis of a unit root if τ_P is less than -4.22 or -3.95, respectively, if τ_P is less than -4.24 or -3.96. We see that the unit root hypothesis cannot be rejected in every case, although for USA and GER, τ_P is close to the critical value for the 10 per cent significance level. Taken together, the result is no longer as clearly in favour of the unit-root hypothesis as in the case of the augmented Dickey-Fuller test. The discussion in the last two sections shows that the Dickey-Fuller test is indeed biased in favour of the null hypothesis of a unit root, and that this problem becomes even more serious if the data generating process is subjected to phenomena like structural breaks. With our short observation period it is not astonishing that this test fails to distinguish between the two types of non-stationarity, because it is designed to detect the long-run characteristics of a time series. A decision between a TS- and a DS-model based on a blind confidence on the results of the Dickey-Fuller test comes close to the automatic use of a difference filter, regardless of the underlying type of non-stationarity. Perron's test is an improvement, but the time consuming model selection procedure prevents this method to be a reasonable alternative for detecting the non-stationarity type for such a huge number of time series as in this study. Furthermore, the reliability of the tests for structural breaks is questionable because of the short observation period. Since the flexibility of the HP-filter prevents this procedure from causing severe distortions if the series contains a (moderate) structural break (see Hillinger et al. (1992b)), it is the method of choice in the case were we assume a TS-model.

Dickey et al. (1986), p. 16 argue that the assumption of a unit root when there is none is not a disadvantage, because this will, in the worst case, 'tend to produce more conservative forecast intervals'. This statement is certainly true from the forecasting point of view, but it is not valid for the description of business cycle stylized facts. The difference filter causes serious distortions to the cyclical structure of the output series if applied in the wrong case, as shown in Section A.1, as well as the HP-filter causes artificial cycles if used with a DS-series. If cyclical structure is found for both filtering methods,

I would put more confidence in ther results for the HP-filter, based on the outcome in Hillinger et al. (1992b). Moreover, the cyclical structure for the HP-filtered series is more similar to the results from the visual examination of the data (see Chapter 2). Given that there is no possibility to detect the non-stationarity type, the following procedure is applied in the study: Both the results for the HP-filtered and the difference filtered series are presented to give the reader the opportunity to chose the appropriate non-stationarity type, and to judge the robustness of the stylized facts with respect to the chosen detrending procedure.

Appendix B

Tables

B.1 Postwar Results

Table B.1: Postwar Results, Univariate Spectra, Cycle Lengths, HP100-Filter

	GDP	GFCF	II	CP	CG	EX	IM	NEX	P	M
AUS	5.87	12.36	7.11	–	–	8.34	5.73	9.76	7.12	12.09
	–	–	3.56	–	–	–	–	3.64	–	3.70
CAN	9.97	8.00	9.80	10.79	–	6.74	6.85	7.61	7.06	10.41
	4.38	–	4.51	–	–	–	–	–	–	2.46
DNK	8.14	9.43	–	8.98	9.34	–	8.68	9.17	6.36	–
	3.04	–	3.92	3.17	2.45	–	3.04	3.20	–	–
FRA	9.40	9.26	–	8.98	8.32	13.34	11.06	9.35	7.28	–
	–	–	–	3.28	3.04	–	3.16	3.46	–	–
GBR	10.43	7.63	–	7.64	6.56	12.67	6.36	5.81	5.70	–
	4.11	–	4.59	–	–	4.65	–	–	–	–
GER	8.10	7.31	6.10	10.12	9.35	6.20	9.03	8.39	9.92	10.71
	–	–	3.38	–	4.24	–	–	3.75	4.47	3.11
ITA	7.58	7.37	6.77	8.40	9.76	–	8.36	9.98	9.16	–
	3.18	–	3.18	3.30	–	–	3.12	3.49	3.79	–
JPN	11.90	11.00	–	–	8.38	5.45	10.12	8.14	6.51	11.32
	3.10	3.24	–	–	2.83	–	3.20	–	–	2.87
NOR	8.04	10.05	5.57	8.88	–	5.72	8.76	7.80	8.20	11.67
	–	4.56	2.68	4.74	–	–	3.22	–	4.35	3.93
SWE	11.83	11.05	5.13	10.19	6.64	7.11	9.32	7.56	9.73	–
	4.12	4.82	–	3.09	–	–	–	–	4.10	–
USA	7.39	7.28	7.52	7.06	10.02	8.95	7.94	11.82	6.76	7.68
	–	2.60	4.15	–	–	–	–	6.76	–	–

First row: long cycle; second row: short cycle.

Table B.2: Postwar Results, Univariate Spectra, Cycle Lengths, Difference Filter

	GDP	GFCF	II	CP	CG	EX	IM	NEX	P	M
AUS	–	10.64	–	–	7.86	–	–	7.44	5.02	–
	4.67	4.15	4.87	4.59	2.35	–	4.57	3.96	–	3.45
CAN	9.62	7.93	5.45	11.68	–	–	8.36	6.23	–	11.28
	3.97	4.17	2.44	4.18	–	4.43	4.32	–	–	2.49
DNK	–	–	–	8.53	–	–	–	8.46	–	–
	3.13	–	3.21	3.14	–	–	2.91	3.12	–	–
FRA	11.12	–	–	–	6.78	–	–	–	–	–
	2.96	–	2.88	–	2.97	–	3.19	–	–	–
GBR	7.04	5.74	5.07	9.05	–	12.54	5.86	–	–	–
	–	–	2.88	2.64	4.60	4.22	–	4.81	–	–
GER	–	6.54	–	7.17	–	–	8.83	8.31	–	8.19
	4.53	–	3.66	–	–	–	3.48	3.82	–	3.01
ITA	6.32	7.16	–	8.27	–	–	6.39	10.21	–	–
	2.90	3.51	3.41	3.18	4.70	–	3.07	3.41	3.54	–
JPN	10.12	12.91	–	–	–	–	9.67	5.89	–	12.59
	2.93	2.92	3.07	–	2.88	3.67	2.97	–	–	2.63
NOR	7.23	6.56	5.39	6.87	–	–	5.89	–	–	12.40
	–	2.66	2.69	2.57	–	4.50	3.05	–	–	3.61
SWE	5.45	10.39	–	–	6.18	–	–	–	–	–
	–	4.03	4.92	–	2.70	4.37	3.19	4.62	–	–
USA	6.33	6.02	–	5.50	–	7.00	6.37	10.54	–	6.94
	–	–	4.99	–	–	–	2.80	5.80	–	2.94

First row: long cycle; second row: short cycle.

Table B.3: Postwar Results, Univariate Spectra, Peak Powers, HP100-Filter

	GDP	GFCF	II	CP	CG	EX	IM	NEX	P	M
AUS	0.16	0.08	0.10	–	–	0.17	0.13	0.21	0.41	0.05
	–	–	0.34	–	–	–	–	0.27	–	0.13
CAN	0.52	0.51	0.15	0.39	–	0.14	0.21	0.22	0.51	0.12
	0.07	–	0.13	–	–	–	–	–	–	0.07
DNK	0.11	0.09	–	0.35	0.34	–	0.10	0.36	0.19	–
	0.15	–	0.19	0.15	0.09	–	0.21	0.15	–	–
FRA	0.18	0.25	–	0.20	0.20	0.09	0.09	0.20	0.26	–
	–	–	–	0.07	0.12	–	0.11	0.14	–	–
GBR	0.32	0.16	–	0.24	0.16	0.22	0.15	0.23	0.21	–
	0.10	–	0.27	–	–	0.09	–	–	–	–
GER	0.16	0.26	0.14	0.22	0.32	0.13	0.24	0.36	0.40	0.12
	–	–	0.24	–	0.08	–	–	0.14	0.24	0.09
ITA	0.25	0.37	0.08	0.40	0.13	–	0.16	0.22	0.23	–
	0.08	–	0.30	0.10	–	–	0.10	0.19	0.08	–
JPN	0.20	0.26	–	–	0.21	0.13	0.13	0.15	0.15	0.16
	0.05	0.04	–	–	0.09	–	0.09	–	–	0.04
NOR	0.33	0.18	0.22	0.40	–	0.19	0.17	0.16	0.24	0.67
	–	0.11	0.18	0.10	–	–	0.08	–	0.12	0.03
SWE	0.19	0.29	0.45	0.30	0.16	0.13	0.09	0.12	0.20	–
	0.17	0.11	–	0.02	–	–	–	–	0.20	–
USA	0.24	0.32	0.09	0.20	0.20	0.13	0.19	0.26	0.23	0.35
	–	0.03	0.20	–	–	–	–	0.12	–	–

First row: long cycle; second row: short cycle.

Table B.4: Postwar Results, Univariate Spectra, Peak Powers, Difference Filter

	GDP	GFCF	II	CP	CG	EX	IM	NEX	P	M
AUS	–	0.07	–	–	0.21	–	–	0.09	0.05	–
	0.14	0.40	0.27	0.21	0.14	–	0.24	0.53	–	0.22
CAN	0.20	0.43	0.10	0.27	–	–	0.09	0.11	–	0.05
	0.16	0.10	0.35	0.09	–	0.14	0.20	–	–	0.21
DNK	–	–	–	0.13	–	–	–	0.13	–	–
	0.24	–	0.31	0.34	–	–	0.34	0.40	–	–
FRA	0.07	–	–	–	0.06	–	–	–	–	–
	0.13	–	0.34	–	0.37	–	0.21	–	–	–
GBR	0.15	0.13	0.27	0.20	–	0.06	0.17	–	–	–
	–	–	0.21	0.09	0.18	0.14	–	0.19	–	–
GER	–	0.14	–	0.14	–	–	0.11	0.23	–	0.05
	0.16	–	0.38	–	–	–	0.14	0.32	–	0.22
ITA	0.13	0.30	–	0.15	–	–	0.06	0.07	–	–
	0.19	0.12	0.22	0.32	0.20	–	0.20	0.32	0.02	–
JPN	0.05	0.11	–	–	–	–	0.06	0.11	–	0.05
	0.15	0.14	0.30	–	0.20	0.20	0.27	–	–	0.16
NOR	0.16	0.09	0.18	0.17	–	–	0.10	–	–	0.20
	–	0.35	0.38	0.14	–	0.21	0.17	–	–	0.10
SWE	0.13	0.06	–	–	0.13	–	–	–	–	–
	–	0.29	0.49	–	0.24	0.17	0.20	0.14	–	–
USA	0.16	0.29	–	0.15	–	0.10	0.14	0.18	–	0.18
	–	–	0.11	–	–	–	0.15	0.14	–	0.10

First row: long cycle; second row: short cycle.

Table B.5: Postwar Results, Univariate Spectra, Moduli, HP100-Filter

	GDP	GFCF	II	CP	CG	EX	IM	NEX	P	M
AUS	0.70	0.55	0.82	–	–	0.76	0.46	0.90	0.89	0.53
	–	–	0.86	–	–	–	–	0.90	–	0.61
CAN	0.96	0.94	0.88	0.93	–	0.61	0.79	0.81	0.92	0.74
	0.82	–	0.82	–	–	–	–	–	–	0.46
DNK	0.70	0.54	–	0.93	0.91	–	0.74	0.94	0.71	–
	0.73	–	0.56	0.83	0.69	–	0.78	0.83	–	–
FRA	0.81	0.85	–	0.83	0.84	0.61	0.67	0.87	0.81	–
	–	–	–	0.67	0.74	–	0.71	0.78	–	–
GBR	0.92	0.69	–	0.80	0.66	0.92	0.65	0.74	0.71	–
	0.82	–	0.73	–	–	0.82	–	–	–	–
GER	0.75	0.81	0.74	0.85	0.91	0.56	0.86	0.92	0.96	0.78
	–	–	0.77	–	0.79	–	–	0.84	0.92	0.70
ITA	0.85	0.89	0.83	0.92	0.68	–	0.79	0.90	0.85	–
	0.66	–	0.85	0.83	–	–	0.67	0.86	0.74	–
JPN	0.86	0.88	–	–	0.84	0.53	0.78	0.68	0.62	0.81
	0.70	0.68	–	–	0.66	–	0.70	–	–	0.54
NOR	0.88	0.89	0.83	0.94	–	0.69	0.80	0.74	0.90	0.98
	–	0.79	0.68	0.81	–	–	0.65	–	0.76	0.76
SWE	0.90	0.92	0.87	0.89	0.69	0.61	0.65	0.59	0.89	–
	0.87	0.83	–	0.55	–	–	–	–	0.87	–
USA	0.82	0.90	0.81	0.75	0.81	0.67	0.78	0.91	0.77	0.89
	–	0.80	0.83	–	–	–	–	0.86	–	–

First row: long cycle; second row: short cycle.

Table B.6: Postwar Results, Univariate Spectra, Moduli, Difference Filter

	GDP	GFCF	II	CP	CG	EX	IM	NEX	P	M
AUS	–	0.87	–	–	0.85	–	–	0.86	0.69	–
	0.64	0.93	0.83	0.65	0.62	–	0.78	0.94	–	0.62
CAN	0.92	0.96	0.72	0.93	–	–	0.84	0.67	–	0.63
	0.85	0.79	0.76	0.82	–	0.47	0.84	–	–	0.64
DNK	–	–	–	0.86	–	–	–	0.89	–	–
	0.65	–	0.66	0.87	–	–	0.74	0.89	–	–
FRA	0.61	–	–	–	0.67	–	–	–	–	–
	0.62	–	0.65	–	0.82	–	0.62	–	–	–
GBR	0.74	0.53	0.86	0.86	–	0.83	0.69	–	–	–
	–	–	0.75	0.84	0.59	0.84	–	0.63	–	–
GER	–	0.60	–	0.63	–	–	0.72	0.90	–	0.49
	0.58	–	0.77	–	–	–	0.72	0.94	–	0.67
ITA	0.69	0.88	–	0.85	–	–	0.48	0.82	–	–
	0.74	0.77	0.74	0.89	0.64	–	0.62	0.89	0.74	–
JPN	0.66	0.79	–	–	–	–	0.67	0.47	–	0.62
	0.72	0.80	0.63	–	0.53	0.55	0.79	–	–	0.62
NOR	0.76	0.76	0.82	0.80	–	–	0.59	–	–	0.93
	–	0.79	0.90	0.62	–	0.65	0.62	–	–	0.79
SWE	0.56	0.85	–	–	0.73	–	–	–	–	–
	–	0.91	0.90	–	0.77	0.55	0.61	0.47	–	–
USA	0.73	0.84	–	0.57	–	0.47	0.61	0.89	–	0.78
	–	–	0.79	–	–	–	0.74	0.87	–	0.59

First row: long cycle; second row: short cycle.

Table B.7: Postwar Results, Univariate Spectra, Signal-to-Noise Ratios, HP100-Filter

	GDP	GFCF	II	CP	CG	EX	IM	NEX	P	M
AUS	5.47	7.99	6.15	–	–	6.86	5.04	11.04	20.06	5.09
CAN	12.05	14.11	5.74	14.98	–	6.34	6.11	6.63	16.27	5.88
DNK	4.89	6.75	4.47	8.75	8.58	–	5.17	8.49	7.63	–
FRA	8.15	13.25	–	7.60	6.33	10.41	5.59	6.24	13.32	–
GBR	13.66	8.78	6.07	13.49	6.97	9.19	7.64	7.63	6.92	–
GER	7.89	13.28	6.64	17.13	10.13	5.40	12.45	10.56	16.96	6.38
ITA	7.05	18.24	6.38	12.92	11.01	–	5.72	6.40	11.83	–
JPN	10.22	12.23	–	–	6.12	4.78	6.55	9.25	6.36	8.16
NOR	9.64	6.12	5.61	10.29	–	6.50	6.40	6.54	6.51	18.09
SWE	13.03	13.84	8.88	12.44	5.57	6.58	5.53	6.65	10.59	–
USA	8.45	11.28	6.63	9.77	20.24	9.83	6.80	23.94	10.05	10.65

Table B.8: Postwar Results, Univariate Spectra, Signal-to-Noise Ratios, Difference Filter

	GDP	GFCF	II	CP	CG	EX	IM	NEX	P	M
AUS	4.23	7.30	11.60	5.18	5.56	–	6.21	10.77	2.64	4.39
CAN	5.91	9.25	5.78	6.82	–	4.22	5.45	4.49	–	4.23
DNK	4.51	–	5.79	5.86	–	–	4.81	6.46	–	–
FRA	4.46	–	6.84	–	5.43	–	4.20	–	–	–
GBR	5.31	4.95	7.67	7.51	4.72	6.51	4.98	5.14	–	–
GER	4.76	6.01	6.70	7.02	–	–	6.32	7.94	–	4.23
ITA	4.67	10.28	9.60	8.24	5.13	–	4.17	5.56	6.08	–
JPN	5.18	6.76	5.85	–	4.09	4.48	4.81	4.65	–	4.27
NOR	4.96	5.04	9.53	4.77	–	5.13	4.29	–	–	5.89
SWE	5.29	6.45	9.09	–	4.81	4.49	4.26	4.26	–	–
USA	4.96	6.53	8.32	5.11	–	5.00	4.51	10.51	–	5.05

Table B.9: Postwar Results, Multivariate Spectra, Cycle Length at Peak of GDP-Autospectrum, HP100-Filter

	GFCF	II	CP	CG	EX	IM	NEX	P	M
AUS	5.45	8.75	7.28	9.42	9.69	9.16	–	5.94	10.51
	–	4.94	–	6.48	5.58	4.97	4.36	–	4.30
CAN	7.45	7.39	8.53	6.88	8.83	8.60	8.25	7.62	8.53
	–	–	–	–	–	–	3.98	–	–
DNK	9.24	7.39	7.80	7.39	7.86	6.09	7.28	8.39	–
	3.45	3.38	–	3.99	4.28	–	2.83	5.02	–
FRA	10.18	9.24	9.24	10.08	8.60	9.98	10.85	11.47	–
	–	3.03	–	–	–	–	4.25	5.87	–
GBR	6.98	8.53	7.34	7.03	7.23	7.45	6.61	7.23	–
	–	–	–	–	–	–	–	–	–
GER	7.45	7.98	7.74	6.52	6.32	7.03	6.09	8.05	7.92
	4.19	4.23	–	–	–	–	–	–	–
ITA	6.65	8.53	6.98	6.61	6.88	6.93	6.93	8.60	–
	–	3.70	–	–	–	–	3.68	–	–
JPN	10.29	11.21	12.32	9.78	13.31	13.86	–	10.85	12.63
	–	3.75	–	–	–	–	3.54	–	4.40
NOR	8.05	7.92	8.25	7.68	7.86	8.39	7.80	7.92	8.05
	–	–	–	–	–	–	–	–	–
SWE	6.70	10.62	7.80	5.34	5.80	9.50	5.84	5.37	–
	–	5.09	–	–	–	5.48	–	–	–
USA	6.40	7.03	6.48	9.42	7.34	6.57	6.93	6.61	7.39
	–	–	–	5.98	–	–	3.26	–	–

Table B.10: Postwar Results, Multivariate Spectra, Cycle Length at Peaks of GDP-Autospectrum, Difference Filter

	GFCF	II	CP	CG	EX	IM	NEX	P	M
AUS	–	–	5.34	5.04	5.31	–	–	5.12	6.28
	4.66	4.44	2.07	–	–	4.73	4.30	–	4.12
CAN	6.57	5.34	8.46	6.79	5.07	9.16	7.56	–	7.80
	3.13	2.37	–	4.46	–	4.56	3.91	–	2.68
DNK	–	6.12	–	5.17	–	–	–	–	–
	3.67	3.36	3.98	3.68	3.72	3.58	4.12	–	–
FRA	7.39	6.70	5.48	6.20	5.34	5.28	6.44	–	–
	4.62	3.11	2.73	3.27	–	3.26	2.92	–	–
GBR	5.07	7.86	7.18	6.05	6.48	5.14	6.48	–	–
	–	2.78	4.30	–	3.55	–	–	–	–
GER	6.28	5.80	–	–	–	–	–	–	5.37
	4.04	3.47	4.30	4.62	4.42	4.19	4.50	–	–
ITA	5.84	7.23	5.77	5.77	5.70	–	6.52	–	–
	3.45	3.37	3.43	3.38	3.43	4.75	3.75	–	–
JPN	11.60	8.60	11.21	10.40	–	–	–	–	10.85
	3.74	3.53	3.66	3.38	3.44	3.63	3.78	–	3.63
NOR	5.77	5.91	6.01	6.12	6.05	6.52	6.05	–	5.87
	–	–	–	–	–	–	–	–	–
SWE	–	–	–	–	5.07	–	5.17	–	–
	4.78	4.97	4.58	4.82	–	4.89	–	–	–
USA	5.74	6.16	5.94	7.34	5.94	6.12	6.61	–	6.20
	–	3.17	3.03	5.04	–	–	–	–	–

Table B.11: Postwar Results, Multivariate Spectra, Squared Coherency, HP100-Filter

	GFCF	II	CP	CG	EX	IM	NEX	P	M
AUS	0.83	0.20	0.75	0.18	0.59	0.24	–	0.50	0.84
	–	0.83	–	0.19	0.35	0.80	0.83	–	0.72
CAN	0.88	0.94	0.93	0.07	0.12	0.78	0.80	0.24	0.88
	–	–	–	–	–	–	0.32	–	–
DNK	0.97	0.69	0.60	0.82	0.38	0.74	0.79	0.45	–
	0.88	0.64	–	0.08	0.24	–	0.85	0.37	–
FRA	0.92	0.93	0.84	0.36	0.60	0.95	0.76	0.74	–
	–	0.85	–	–	–	–	0.06	0.10	–
GBR	0.84	0.98	0.91	0.52	0.47	0.81	0.66	0.78	–
	–	–	–	–	–	–	–	–	–
GER	0.92	0.89	0.94	0.62	0.04	0.94	0.19	0.65	0.58
	–	0.71	–	–	–	–	–	–	–
ITA	0.93	0.62	0.95	0.65	0.70	0.73	0.46	0.82	–
	–	0.92	–	–	–	–	0.70	–	–
JPN	0.87	0.95	0.89	0.54	0.50	0.55	–	0.77	0.87
	–	0.87	–	–	–	–	0.19	–	0.31
NOR	0.40	0.75	0.90	0.04	0.23	0.76	0.16	0.81	0.47
	–	–	–	–	–	–	–	–	–
SWE	0.80	0.77	0.57	0.45	0.76	0.89	0.81	0.83	–
	–	0.93	–	–	–	0.81	–	–	–
USA	0.96	0.91	0.94	0.67	0.79	0.91	0.88	0.86	0.58
	–	–	–	0.19	–	–	0.61	–	–

sc between the GDP cycle and the cycle in the other series
First row: long cycle; second row: short cycle.

Table B.12: Postwar Results, Multivariate Spectra, Squared Coherency, Difference Filter

	GFCF	II	CP	CG	EX	IM	NEX	P	M
AUS	–	–	0.84	0.26	0.22	–	–	0.01	0.48
	0.82	0.74	0.31	–	–	0.82	0.68	–	0.68
CAN	0.83	0.86	0.95	0.07	0.54	0.76	0.72	–	0.63
	0.83	0.71	–	0.59	–	0.84	0.35	–	0.66
DNK	–	0.61	–	0.75	–	–	–	–	–
	0.88	0.71	0.75	0.07	0.29	0.81	0.57	–	–
FRA	0.83	0.84	0.65	0.40	0.74	0.67	0.67	–	–
	0.77	0.89	0.75	0.68	–	0.73	0.81	–	–
GBR	0.52	0.86	0.88	0.33	0.52	0.89	0.65	–	–
	–	0.90	0.70	–	0.67	–	–	–	–
GER	0.93	0.84	–	–	–	–	–	–	0.36
	0.79	0.86	0.74	0.55	0.33	0.72	0.02	–	–
ITA	0.89	0.60	0.90	0.60	0.65	–	0.48	–	–
	0.69	0.96	0.89	0.58	0.06	0.67	0.71	–	–
JPN	0.93	0.74	0.80	0.52	–	–	–	–	0.83
	0.91	0.87	0.83	0.40	0.43	0.68	0.17	–	0.73
NOR	0.14	0.76	0.66	0.04	0.73	0.46	0.08	–	0.06
	–	–	–	–	–	–	–	–	–
SWE	–	–	–	–	0.78	–	0.75	–	–
	0.33	0.97	0.16	0.41	–	0.89	–	–	–
USA	0.95	0.83	0.97	0.41	0.72	0.86	0.83	–	0.31
	–	0.81	0.60	0.20	–	–	–	–	–

sc between the GDP cycle and the cycle in the other series
First row: long cycle; second row: short cycle.

Table B.13: Postwar Results, Multivariate Spectra, Phase Shift, HP100-Filter

	GFCF	II	CP	CG	EX	IM	NEX	P	M
AUS	-0.18	-0.88	-0.51	2.38	-0.09	-2.38	–	-0.75	-2.53
	–	0.32	–	-2.02	1.81	-0.10	2.10	–	0.29
CAN	-0.95	0.77	-0.23	-1.70	2.39	-1.12	2.75	-2.31	-0.20
	–	–	–	–	–	–	-1.61	–	–
DNK	-0.32	1.49	0.17	3.37	3.85	-0.05	-3.60	2.94	–
	0.06	-0.29	–	1.64	-0.33	–	-1.35	-2.45	–
FRA	0.22	1.38	0.22	-0.02	-1.09	0.33	-3.81	-4.50	–
	–	-0.17	–	–	–	–	0.05	2.59	–
GBR	-0.07	1.09	-0.40	-2.45	0.17	-0.10	2.83	-2.67	–
	–	–	–	–	–	–	–	–	–
GER	-0.10	1.66	0.10	-1.19	-1.64	0.18	-2.47	-1.56	0.26
	–	0.17	–	–	–	–	–	–	–
ITA	-0.30	1.95	-0.51	0.97	1.23	-0.38	2.55	-3.90	–
	–	0.10	–	–	–	–	-1.69	–	–
JPN	-0.17	0.95	-0.40	-2.22	0.17	-1.36	–	-5.07	-3.09
	–	-0.55	–	–	–	–	1.37	–	0.92
NOR	0.32	1.36	0.19	1.34	1.39	1.21	-3.57	3.33	-1.13
	–	–	–	–	–	–	–	–	–
SWE	-0.50	-0.29	-1.06	-0.48	1.05	-0.81	2.17	-1.75	–
	–	-0.25	–	–	–	-0.03	–	–	–
USA	0.15	1.10	0.23	-0.32	-1.64	0.46	-2.27	-2.79	0.36
	–	–	–	-1.95	–	–	1.37	–	–

Phase lead of the GDP cycle over the cycle in the other series
First row: long cycle; second row: short cycle.

Table B.14: Postwar Results, Multivariate Spectra, Phase Shift, Difference Filter

	GFCF	II	CP	CG	EX	IM	NEX	P	M
AUS	–	–	-0.01	-1.52	1.36	–	–	0.09	-0.46
	-0.44	0.22	-0.05	–	–	-0.14	2.02	–	0.27
CAN	-0.86	0.67	-0.08	-0.98	0.10	-0.48	2.81	–	0.02
	0.04	-0.22	–	-0.06	–	0.07	-1.62	–	0.95
DNK	–	1.24	–	2.14	–	–	–	–	–
	0.06	-0.32	-0.19	-1.30	-0.31	-0.38	1.88	–	–
FRA	-0.22	0.82	0.27	1.19	-0.29	0.37	-2.17	–	–
	0.06	-0.18	0.32	1.09	–	0.17	-1.32	–	–
GBR	-0.27	0.81	-0.34	-2.28	0.24	-0.01	2.77	–	–
	–	-0.27	0.25	–	-0.63	–	–	–	–
GER	-0.11	0.81	–	–	–	–	–	–	0.76
	0.12	0.19	-0.29	-1.39	-0.17	-0.13	-1.62	–	–
ITA	-0.25	1.23	-0.54	1.02	1.20	–	2.45	–	–
	-0.01	0.08	0.14	-1.67	-1.47	0.02	-1.71	–	–
JPN	-0.37	0.62	-0.37	-2.54	–	–	–	–	-2.83
	0.04	-0.52	0.16	1.06	-1.26	-0.17	1.64	–	0.82
NOR	-2.00	0.43	-0.20	2.08	0.83	0.84	1.90	–	-1.54
	–	–	–	–	–	–	–	–	–
SWE	–	–	–	–	1.01	–	2.01	–	–
	-0.61	-0.28	0.15	-0.07	–	0.03	–	–	–
USA	0.10	0.64	0.27	-0.84	-1.18	0.40	-2.10	–	0.33
	–	-0.04	0.28	-2.15	–	–	–	–	–

Phase lead of the GDP cycle over the cycle in the other series
First row: long cycle; second row: short cycle.

Table B.15: Postwar Results, Multivariate Spectra, Gain, HP100-Filter

	GFCF	II	CP	CG	EX	IM	NEX	P	M
AUS	0.26	3.02	0.77	0.23	0.28	0.28	–	0.58	0.36
	–	1.54	–	0.40	0.26	0.17	0.86	–	0.30
CAN	0.34	4.74	0.81	0.57	0.20	0.56	2.02	0.40	0.68
	–	–	–	–	–	–	1.36	–	–
DNK	0.17	3.98	0.39	0.11	0.34	0.45	0.87	0.55	–
	0.31	1.48	–	0.05	0.51	–	0.64	1.02	–
FRA	0.26	4.40	1.20	1.13	0.23	0.28	1.57	0.34	–
	–	0.91	–	–	–	–	0.29	0.29	–
GBR	0.35	5.81	0.68	1.01	0.73	0.49	1.49	0.69	–
	–	–	–	–	–	–	–	–	–
GER	0.28	4.50	0.72	0.64	0.13	0.31	0.76	0.82	0.52
	–	2.20	–	–	–	–	–	–	–
ITA	0.29	5.91	0.92	1.87	0.41	0.30	1.27	0.49	–
	–	1.45	–	–	–	–	1.35	–	–
JPN	0.32	11.69	1.63	1.83	0.57	0.31	–	0.65	0.49
	–	2.54	–	–	–	–	0.68	–	0.30
NOR	0.20	2.55	0.67	0.61	0.51	0.38	0.43	0.67	0.32
	–	–	–	–	–	–	–	–	–
SWE	0.36	2.84	0.61	0.89	0.38	0.38	0.94	1.01	–
	–	0.88	–	–	–	0.43	–	–	–
USA	0.29	6.84	1.17	0.42	0.34	0.33	2.67	1.52	0.59
	–	–	–	0.61	–	–	4.35	–	–

Amplitude of the GDP cycle in per cent of the amplitude of the cycle in the other series
First row: long cycle; second row: short cycle.

Table B.16: Postwar Results, Multivariate Spectra, Gain, Difference Filter

	GFCF	II	CP	CG	EX	IM	NEX	P	M
AUS	–	–	0.75	0.56	0.24	–	–	0.15	0.34
	0.31	1.41	0.99	–	–	0.18	0.73	–	0.27
CAN	0.24	3.02	0.85	0.31	0.26	0.36	1.85	–	0.57
	0.55	1.29	–	0.51	–	0.24	1.32	–	0.32
DNK	–	2.93	–	0.11	–	–	–	–	–
	0.30	1.76	0.72	0.05	0.59	0.34	0.98	–	–
FRA	0.23	3.40	1.09	0.99	0.28	0.27	1.35	–	–
	0.47	0.96	0.93	0.70	–	0.14	0.89	–	–
GBR	0.27	4.66	0.74	0.79	0.77	0.40	1.47	–	–
	–	1.47	0.92	–	0.39	–	–	–	–
GER	0.28	2.56	–	–	–	–	–	–	0.55
	0.56	1.12	1.22	1.20	0.35	0.44	0.21	–	–
ITA	0.27	5.25	1.11	1.74	0.40	–	1.32	–	–
	0.48	1.32	0.92	2.04	0.13	0.30	1.37	–	–
JPN	0.38	6.77	1.50	1.61	–	–	–	–	0.46
	0.43	2.49	0.83	0.95	0.18	0.18	0.59	–	0.50
NOR	0.13	1.30	0.56	0.55	0.59	0.30	0.29	–	0.17
	–	–	–	–	–	–	–	–	–
SWE	–	–	–	–	0.36	–	0.88	–	–
	0.29	0.90	0.59	0.74	–	0.36	–	–	–
USA	0.30	5.71	1.27	0.38	0.33	0.35	2.65	–	0.53
	–	1.57	1.00	0.69	–	–	–	–	–

Amplitude of the GDP cycle in per cent of the amplitude of the cycle in the other series
First row: long cycle; second row: short cycle.

B.2   Prewar Results

Table B.17: Prewar Results, Univariate Spectra, Cycle Lengths, HP100-Filter

	Y1	Y2	Y3	I	CP	CG	NEX	P1	P2	P3	M
AUS	10.58	–	–	–	–	–	–	10.22	–	–	0.00
	–	–	–	–	–	–	–	3.40	–	–	4.44
CAN	8.51	7.39	7.02	8.41	–	8.74	5.81	8.45	8.68	8.28	8.68
	2.78	–	–	–	–	2.42	2.80	–	–	–	3.52
DNK	7.74	–	–	7.90	–	–	–	8.54	–	–	8.00
	2.94	–	–	–	–	–	–	–	–	–	3.34
GBR	7.55	–	–	10.10	–	11.80	–	8.82	–	–	8.97
	–	–	–	–	–	4.98	–	3.83	–	–	–
GER	9.47	–	–	–	–	–	–	8.45	–	–	0.00
	–	–	–	–	–	–	–	–	–	–	–
ITA	5.55	–	–	–	–	–	–	5.42	–	–	8.87
	–	–	–	–	–	–	–	–	–	–	–
JPN	5.65	–	–	9.71	–	6.40	7.73	6.47	–	–	0.00
	2.55	–	–	2.83	–	–	3.81	–	–	–	–
NOR	9.86	–	–	8.57	–	8.73	–	8.57	–	–	9.29
	–	–	–	–	–	–	–	–	–	–	3.01
SWE	8.82	–	–	11.08	8.55	8.06	–	7.84	–	–	9.57
	3.19	–	–	3.79	3.44	–	–	–	–	–	2.20
USA	7.50	5.43	–	7.17	–	7.48	9.93	8.63	8.76	8.78	9.32
	–	–	–	2.59	–	4.04	4.73	2.55	2.51	3.10	–

First row: long cycle; second row: short cycle.

Table B.18: Prewar Results, Univariate Spectra, Cycle Lengths, Difference Filter

	Y1	Y2	Y3	I	CP	CG	NEX	P1	P2	P3	M
AUS	11.36	–	–	–	–	–	–	–	–	–	0.00
	2.23	–	–	–	–	–	–	–	–	–	3.45
CAN	5.83	–	–	–	–	–	5.79	6.15	7.92	7.28	0.00
	–	–	–	–	–	–	2.75	–	–	–	–
DNK	6.93	–	–	–	–	–	–	8.26	–	–	7.52
	2.66	–	–	–	–	–	–	2.66	–	–	2.88
GBR	6.41	–	–	–	–	6.65	–	–	–	–	14.18
	2.59	–	–	–	3.28	–	–	–	–	–	–
GER	–	–	–	–	–	–	–	7.45	–	–	–
	–	–	–	–	–	–	–	–	–	–	–
ITA	–	–	–	–	–	–	–	–	–	–	0.00
	4.02	–	–	–	–	–	–	4.37	–	–	–
JPN	–	–	–	–	–	5.44	7.23	–	–	–	0.00
	4.49	–	–	–	–	–	3.63	–	–	–	–
NOR	5.12	–	–	–	–	–	–	–	–	–	0.00
	–	–	–	–	–	–	3.07	–	–	–	–
SWE	–	–	–	10.68	–	–	–	6.31	–	–	11.39
	3.14	–	–	3.65	–	–	–	–	–	–	2.47
USA	–	–	–	–	–	–	8.49	7.68	7.82	–	0.00
	4.09	–	–	2.57	–	4.40	3.89	2.52	2.49	–	–

First row: long cycle; second row: short cycle.

Table B.19: Prewar Results, Univariate Spectra, Peak Power, HP100-Filter

	Y1	Y2	Y3	I	CP	CG	NEX	P1	P2	P3	M
AUS	0.21	–	–	–	–	–	–	0.27	–	–	0.00
	–	–	–	–	–	–	–	0.08	–	–	0.11
CAN	0.16	0.18	0.17	0.20	–	0.29	0.61	0.25	0.39	0.27	0.47
	0.07	–	–	–	–	0.07	0.04	–	–	–	0.06
DNK	0.38	–	–	0.26	–	–	–	0.38	–	–	0.53
	0.05	–	–	–	–	–	–	–	–	–	0.03
GBR	0.27	–	–	0.12	–	0.21	–	0.64	–	–	0.36
	–	–	–	–	–	0.17	–	0.02	–	–	–
GER	0.11	–	–	–	–	–	–	0.28	–	–	0.00
	–	–	–	–	–	–	–	–	–	–	–
ITA	0.11	–	–	–	–	–	–	0.23	–	–	0.19
	–	–	–	–	–	–	–	–	–	–	–
JPN	0.15	–	–	0.19	–	0.21	0.25	0.19	–	–	0.00
	0.19	–	–	0.10	–	–	0.19	–	–	–	–
NOR	0.12	–	–	0.13	–	0.14	–	0.36	–	–	0.41
	–	–	–	–	–	–	–	–	–	–	0.03
SWE	0.16	–	–	0.26	0.20	0.19	–	0.21	–	–	0.51
	0.11	–	–	0.12	0.11	–	–	–	–	–	0.06
USA	0.11	0.14	–	0.08	–	0.07	0.13	0.27	0.28	0.18	0.16
	–	–	–	0.20	–	0.36	0.09	0.07	0.06	0.07	–

First row: long cycle; second row: short cycle.

Table B.20: Prewar Results, Univariate Spectra, Peak Power, Difference Filter

	Y1	Y2	Y3	I	CP	CG	NEX	P1	P2	P3	M
AUS	0.05	–	–	–	–	–	–	–	–	–	0.00
	0.33	–	–	–	–	–	–	–	–	–	0.23
CAN	0.08	–	–	–	–	–	0.46	0.16	0.17	0.11	0.00
	–	–	–	–	–	–	0.16	–	–	–	–
DNK	0.24	–	–	–	–	–	–	0.21	–	–	0.36
	0.14	–	–	–	–	–	–	0.11	–	–	0.10
GBR	0.18	–	–	–	–	0.13	–	–	–	–	0.08
	0.11	–	–	–	0.19	–	–	–	–	–	–
GER	–	–	–	–	–	–	–	0.14	–	–	0.00
	–	–	–	–	–	–	–	–	–	–	–
ITA	–	–	–	–	–	–	–	–	–	–	0.00
	0.10	–	–	–	–	–	–	0.20	–	–	–
JPN	–	–	–	–	–	0.23	0.10	–	–	–	0.00
	0.10	–	–	–	–	–	0.23	–	–	–	–
NOR	0.13	–	–	–	–	–	–	–	–	–	0.00
	–	–	–	–	–	–	0.20	–	–	–	–
SWE	–	–	–	0.06	–	–	–	0.14	–	–	0.10
	0.21	–	–	0.23	–	–	–	–	–	–	0.24
USA	–	–	–	–	–	–	0.06	0.12	0.13	–	0.00
	0.13	–	–	0.28	–	0.22	0.09	0.26	0.24	–	–

First row: long cycle; second row: short cycle.

Table B.21: Prewar Results, Univariate Spectra, Modulus, HP100-Filter

	Y1	Y2	Y3	I	CP	CG	NEX	P1	P2	P3	M
AUS	0.86	–	–	–	–	–	–	0.90	–	–	0.00
	–	–	–	–	–	–	–	0.72	–	–	0.61
CAN	0.78	0.76	0.73	0.79	–	0.88	0.95	0.87	0.91	0.85	0.94
	0.52	–	–	–	–	0.58	0.95	–	–	–	0.75
DNK	0.90	–	–	0.83	–	–	–	0.90	–	–	0.94
	0.62	–	–	–	–	–	–	–	–	–	0.64
GBR	0.85	–	–	0.68	–	0.90	–	0.96	–	–	0.89
	–	–	–	–	–	0.88	–	0.68	–	–	–
GER	0.72	–	–	–	–	–	–	0.86	–	–	0.00
	–	–	–	–	–	–	–	–	–	–	–
ITA	0.59	–	–	–	–	–	–	0.72	–	–	0.79
	–	–	–	–	–	–	–	–	–	–	–
JPN	0.60	–	–	0.84	–	0.74	0.94	0.71	–	–	0.00
	0.76	–	–	0.72	–	–	0.86	–	–	–	–
NOR	0.69	–	–	0.65	–	0.74	–	0.90	–	–	0.92
	–	–	–	–	–	–	–	–	–	–	0.66
SWE	0.80	–	–	0.93	0.87	0.77	–	0.77	–	–	0.95
	0.71	–	–	0.81	0.73	–	–	–	–	–	0.61
USA	0.66	0.56	–	0.64	–	0.82	0.85	0.88	0.88	0.81	0.74
	–	–	–	0.68	–	0.88	0.75	0.60	0.59	0.62	–

First row: long cycle; second row: short cycle.

Table B.22: Prewar Results, Univariate Spectra, Modulus, Difference Filter

	Y1	Y2	Y3	I	CP	CG	NEX	P1	P2	P3	M
AUS	0.65	–	–	–	–	–	–	–	–	–	0.00
	0.68	–	–	–	–	–	–	–	–	–	0.72
CAN	0.51	–	–	–	–	–	0.96	0.75	0.78	0.67	0.00
	–	–	–	–	–	–	0.92	–	–	–	–
DNK	0.86	–	–	–	–	–	–	0.85	–	–	0.91
	0.70	–	–	–	–	–	–	0.66	–	–	0.75
GBR	0.78	–	–	–	–	0.57	–	–	–	–	0.58
	0.52	–	–	–	0.46	–	–	–	–	–	–
GER	–	–	–	–	–	–	–	0.74	–	–	0.00
	–	–	–	–	–	–	–	–	–	–	–
ITA	–	–	–	–	–	–	–	–	–	–	0.00
	0.55	–	–	–	–	–	–	0.62	–	–	–
JPN	–	–	–	–	–	0.75	0.88	–	–	–	0.00
	0.63	–	–	–	–	–	0.88	–	–	–	–
NOR	0.64	–	–	–	–	–	–	–	–	–	0.00
	–	–	–	–	–	–	0.45	–	–	–	–
SWE	–	–	–	0.87	–	–	–	0.58	–	–	0.77
	0.65	–	–	0.87	–	–	–	–	–	–	0.81
USA	–	–	–	–	–	–	0.79	0.75	0.73	–	0.00
	0.51	–	–	0.49	–	0.70	0.86	0.80	0.81	–	–

First row: long cycle; second row: short cycle.

Table B.23: Prewar Results, Univariate Spectra, Signal-to-Noise Ratio, HP100-Filter

	Y1	Y2	Y3	I	CP	CG	NEX	P1	P2	P3	M
AUS	7.80	–	–	–	–	–	–	7.00	–	–	6.41
CAN	5.59	6.11	5.44	8.68	–	7.60	12.70	8.52	15.67	9.47	10.35
DNK	9.03	–	–	10.45	–	–	–	11.89	–	–	16.19
GBR	7.99	–	–	11.24	–	12.91	–	18.15	–	–	10.43
GER	4.95	–	–	–	–	–	–	10.22	–	–	–
ITA	4.20	–	–	–	–	–	–	6.77	–	–	11.95
JPN	4.74	–	–	6.39	–	8.44	7.01	7.74	–	–	–
NOR	8.85	–	–	8.78	–	6.04	–	12.80	–	–	12.68
SWE	6.30	–	–	6.23	5.41	7.37	–	12.27	–	–	14.44
USA	4.43	4.99	–	4.14	–	6.77	5.20	7.18	7.49	6.50	13.15

Table B.24: Prewar Results, Univariate Spectra, Signal-to-Noise Ratio, Difference Filter

	Y1	Y2	Y3	I	CP	CG	NEX	P1	P2	P3	M
AUS	4.85	–	–	–	–	–	–	–	–	–	5.00
CAN	4.01	–	–	–	–	–	16.41	4.91	6.02	4.57	–
DNK	5.54	–	–	–	–	–	–	5.68	–	–	7.96
GBR	4.79	–	–	–	4.37	5.84	–	–	–	–	9.33
GER	–	–	–	–	–	–	–	5.16	–	–	–
ITA	5.54	–	–	–	–	–	–	4.87	–	–	–
JPN	6.02	–	–	–	–	5.48	7.95	–	–	–	–
NOR	4.71	–	–	–	–	–	4.49	–	–	–	–
SWE	4.36	–	–	5.66	–	–	–	5.68	–	–	5.67
USA	4.39	–	–	4.92	–	7.79	6.48	4.80	4.82	–	–

Table B.25: Prewar Results, Multivariate Spectra, Cycle Length at Peaks of GDP-Autospectrum, HP100-Filter

	I	CP	CG	NEX	P	M
AUS	10.29	–	–	11.34	10.18	–
	–	–	–	–	–	–
CAN	8.75	–	9.07	6.16	8.39	7.50
	2.31	–	3.63	–	4.52	–
DNK	7.56	–	–	–	7.50	7.92
	6.09	–	–	–	–	–
GBR	7.92	7.18	7.23	–	8.05	–
	–	–	–	–	–	–
GER	–	–	–	–	9.33	–
	–	–	–	–	2.05	–
ITA	6.01	–	–	–	5.80	–
	–	–	–	–	–	–
JPN	–	–	6.96	–	6.44	–
	4.66	4.80	4.92	–	–	4.97
NOR	9.60	9.88	9.78	9.98	8.46	–
	4.36	–	–	–	–	–
SWE	9.88	7.50	7.34	7.68	7.68	–
	–	–	–	–	–	–
USA	–	–	–	–	8.32	9.78
	–	–	–	–	2.44	4.60

Table B.26: Prewar Results, Multivariate Spectra, Cycle Length at Peaks of GDP-Autospectrum, Difference Filter

	I	CP	CG	NEX	P	M
AUS	–	–	–	–	7.72	–
	–	–	–	–	–	–
CAN	7.45	–	7.23	6.57	7.68	7.68
	4.07	–	2.99	3.84	3.82	3.82
DNK	5.17	–	–	–	6.52	6.12
	–	–	–	–	2.52	–
GBR	7.08	6.24	6.16	–	7.03	–
	4.97	2.86	–	–	–	–
GER	–	–	–	–	–	–
	–	–	–	–	–	–
ITA	–	–	–	–	–	–
	4.75	–	–	–	4.21	–
JPN	–	–	–	–	6.57	–
	3.62	–	4.66	–	3.51	4.11
NOR	7.80	6.65	8.60	6.65	7.80	–
	4.07	–	4.84	4.23	4.60	–
SWE	–	–	–	–	5.31	–
	3.44	3.35	3.37	3.58	3.33	–
USA	–	–	–	–	–	8.05
	–	–	–	–	4.01	3.85

Table B.27: Prewar Results, Multivariate Spectra, Squared Coherency, HP100-Filter

	I	CP	CG	NEX	P	M
AUS	0.54	–	–	0.62	0.86	–
	–	–	–	–	–	–
CAN	0.91	–	0.94	0.96	0.88	0.88
	0.27	–	0.26	–	0.36	–
DNK	0.78	–	–	–	0.76	0.59
	0.21	–	–	–	–	–
GBR	0.63	0.20	0.33	–	0.82	–
	–	–	–	–	–	–
GER	–	–	–	–	–	–
	–	–	–	–	0.17	–
ITA	0.51	–	–	–	0.12	–
	–	–	–	–	–	–
JPN	–	–	0.43	–	0.75	–
	0.20	0.33	0.82	–	–	0.33
NOR	0.95	0.91	0.56	0.63	0.76	–
	0.25	–	–	–	–	–
SWE	0.72	0.76	0.33	0.51	0.51	–
	–	–	–	–	–	–
USA	–	–	–	–	0.57	0.80
	–	–	–	–	0.14	0.35

sc between the output cycle and the cycle in the other series
First row: long cycle; second row: short cycle.

Table B.28: Prewar Results, Multivariate Spectra, Squared Coherency, Difference Filter

	I	CP	CG	NEX	P	M
AUS	–	–	–	–	–	–
	0.13	–	–	0.27	–	–
CAN	0.86	–	0.77	0.97	–	0.78
	0.21	–	0.22	0.31	–	0.54
DNK	0.25	–	–	–	–	0.11
	–	–	–	–	–	–
GBR	0.45	0.24	0.16	–	–	–
	0.28	0.69	–	–	–	–
GER	–	–	–	–	–	–
	–	–	–	–	0.01	–
ITA	–	–	–	–	–	–
	0.54	–	–	–	–	–
JPN	–	–	–	–	–	–
	0.13	-1.00	0.83	–	–	0.39
NOR	0.88	0.84	0.49	0.47	–	–
	0.38	–	0.39	0.51	–	–
SWE	–	–	–	–	–	–
	0.50	0.62	0.21	0.05	–	–
USA	–	–	–	–	–	0.65
	–	–	–	–	–	0.60

sc between the output cycle and the cycle in the other series
First row: long cycle; second row: short cycle.

Table B.29: Prewar Results, Multivariate Spectra, Phase Shift, HP100-Filter

	I	CP	CG	NEX	P	M
AUS	-0.21	–	–	-4.30	0.39	–
	–	–	–	–	–	–
CAN	-0.48	–	-3.49	-2.83	0.01	0.26
	-0.27	–	-1.69	–	-2.10	–
DNK	-0.18	–	–	–	-1.36	-0.78
	-0.27	–	–	–	–	–
GBR	-1.64	-1.20	-1.86	–	-0.96	–
	–	–	–	–	–	–
GER	–	–	–	–	-3.83	–
	–	–	–	–	0.09	–
ITA	0.26	–	–	–	1.85	–
	–	–	–	–	–	–
JPN	–	–	-1.77	–	-2.61	–
	-1.75	0.62	-0.16	–	–	1.67
NOR	0.52	-0.57	-2.30	-4.68	0.33	–
	-0.75	–	–	–	–	–
SWE	-0.90	-0.50	1.78	2.07	-1.92	–
	–	–	–	–	–	–
USA	–	–	–	–	-1.44	-1.64
	–	–	–	–	-0.60	0.45

Phase lead of the output cycle over the cycle in the other series
First row: long cycle; second row: short cycle.

Table B.30: Prewar Results, Multivariate Spectra, Phase Shift, Difference Filter

	I	CP	CG	NEX	P	M
AUS	–	–	–	–	–	–
	0.43	–	–	-0.08	–	–
CAN	-0.34	–	-2.92	-2.99	–	0.11
	0.07	–	-1.32	1.42	–	-1.81
DNK	0.23	–	–	–	–	-0.18
	–	–	–	–	–	–
GBR	-1.53	-0.76	-1.57	–	–	–
	0.61	0.22	–	–	–	–
GER	–	–	–	–	–	–
	–	–	–	–	-0.62	–
ITA	–	–	–	–	–	–
	0.24	–	–	–	–	–
JPN	–	–	–	–	–	–
	-1.73	-1.00	-0.17	–	–	1.59
NOR	0.42	-0.45	-2.24	3.11	–	–
	-0.81	–	1.48	0.49	–	–
SWE	–	–	–	–	–	–
	0.20	-0.14	1.10	-0.07	–	–
USA	–	–	–	–	–	-1.42
	–	–	–	–	–	0.39

Phase lead of the output cycle over the cycle in the other series
First row: long cycle; second row: short cycle.

Table B.31: Prewar Results, Multivariate Spectra, Gain, HP100-Filter

	I	CP	CG	NEX	P	M
AUS	0.46	–	–	2.42	1.56	–
	–	–	–	–	–	–
CAN	0.27	–	0.40	1.36	1.14	0.62
	0.24	–	0.32	–	0.79	–
DNK	0.22	–	–	–	1.12	0.35
	0.19	–	–	–	–	–
GBR	0.23	1.53	0.15	–	0.71	–
	–	–	–	–	–	–
GER	–	–	–	–	0.03	–
	–	–	–	–	0.65	–
ITA	0.11	–	–	–	0.16	–
	–	–	–	–	–	–
JPN	–	–	0.05	–	0.25	–
	0.18	0.62	0.10	–	–	0.13
NOR	0.27	0.90	0.28	1.71	0.32	–
	0.15	–	–	–	–	–
SWE	0.14	0.88	0.24	1.17	0.31	–
	–	–	–	–	–	–
USA	–	–	–	–	0.77	0.44
	–	–	–	–	0.73	0.72

Amplitude of the output cycle in per cent of the amplitude of the cycle in the other series
First row: long cycle; second row: short cycle.

Table B.32: Prewar Results, Multivariate Spectra, Gain, Difference Filter

	I	CP	CG	NEX	P	M
AUS	–	–	–	–	–	–
	0.10	–	–	1.03	–	–
CAN	0.26	–	0.42	1.55	–	1.02
	0.21	–	0.29	1.90	–	1.18
DNK	0.18	–	–	–	–	0.19
	–	–	–	–	–	–
GBR	0.19	1.43	0.10	–	–	–
	0.19	0.75	–	–	–	–
GER	–	–	–	–	–	–
	–	–	–	–	0.06	–
ITA	–	–	–	–	–	–
	0.11	–	–	–	–	–
JPN	–	–	–	–	–	–
	0.15	–	0.09	–	–	0.15
NOR	0.26	0.85	0.29	1.38	–	–
	0.18	–	0.27	0.71	–	–
SWE	–	–	–	–	–	–
	0.12	0.92	0.41	0.47	–	–
USA	–	–	–	–	–	0.46
	–	–	–	–	–	1.15

Amplitude of the output cycle in per cent of the amplitude of the cycle in the other series
First row: long cycle; second row: short cycle.

References

Ables, J. G.: 1974, Maximum Entropy spectral analysis, *Astronomy and Astrophysics Supplement Series* **15**, 383–393. Reprinted in (Childers 1978), pp. 23-33.

Abramovitz, M.: 1964, *Evidence of Long Swings in Aggregate Construction since the Civil War*, National Bureau of Economic Research, New York.

Akaike, H.: 1969, Power spectrum estimation through autoregressive modell fitting, *Annals of the Institue of Statistical Mathematics* **21**(407-419), 407–419.

Altman, M.: 1992, Revised real Canadian GNP estimates and Canadian economic growth, *Review of Income and Wealth* **38**, 455–473.

Backus, D. K. and Kehoe, P. J.: 1992, International evidence on the historical properties of business cycles, *American Economic Review* **82**, 864–888.

Balke, N. S. and Gordon, R. J.: 1986, Appendix B: Historical data, *in* R. J. Gordon (ed.), *The American Business Cycle. Continuity and Change*, University of Chicago Press, Chicago and London, pp. 781–850.

Balke, N. S. and Gordon, R. J.: 1989, The estimation of prewar gross national product: Methodology and new evidence, *Journal of Political Economy* **97**, 38–92.

Baxter, M.: 1991, Business cycles, stylized facts, and the exchange rate regime: Evidence from the United States, *Journal of International Money and Finance* **10**, 71–88.

Baxter, M. and Stockman, A. C.: 1989, Business cycles and the exchange-rate regime. Some international evidence, *Journal of Monetary Economics* **23**, 377–400.

Beckstein, W.: 1987, National income, *in* J. Eatwell, M. Milgate and P. Newman (eds), *The New Palgrave. A Dictionary of Economics*, Vol. 3, Macmillan, London, Basingstoke, pp. 590–592.

Beveridge, W. H.: 1921, Weather and harvest cycles, *Economic Journal* **31**, 429–452.

Blackburn, K. and Ravn, M. O.: 1992, Business cycles in the United Kingdom: Facts and fictions, *Economica* **59**, 383–401.

Bloomfield, P.: 1976, *Fourier Analysis of Time Series: An Introduction*, John Wiley & Sons, New York, London, Sidney, Toronto.

Borchardt, K.: 1976, Wandlungen des Konjunkturphänomens in den letzten hundert Jahren, *Bayerische Akademie der Wissenschaften, Sitzungsberichte der Philosophisch-historischen Klasse*. Reprinted in Borchardt (1982), pp. 28-70.

Borchardt, K.: 1982, *Wachstum, Krisen, Handlungsspielräume der Wirtschaftspolitik*, Vandenhoeck & Rupprecht, Göttingen.

Bowden, R. J. and Martin, V. L.: 1992, No, business cycles are not all alike: The United States and Australia compared, *Australian Economic Papers* **31**, 385–398.

Box, G. E. and Jenkins, G. M.: 1970, *Time Series Analysis. Forecasting and Control*, Holden–Day, San Fransico, Cambridge, London, Amsterdam.

Brandner, P. and Neusser, K.: 1992, Business cycles in open economies: Stylized facts for Austria and Germany, *Weltwirtschaftliches Archiv* **128**, 67–87.

Brockwell, P. J. and Davis, R. A.: 1991, *Time Series: Theory and Methods*, 2nd edn, Springer, Berlin, Heidelberg, New York, Tokio.

Brown, R., Durbin, J. and Evans, J.: 1975, Techniques for testing the constancy of regression relationships over time, *Journal of the Royal Statistical Society* **37**, 149–192.

Burg, J. P.: 1967, Maximum entropy spectral analysis, *Proceedings of the 37th Meeting of the Society of Exploration Geophysicists*. Reprinted in Childers (1978), pp. 34-41.

Burg, J. P.: 1968, A new analysis technique for time series data, *NATO Advanced Study Institute on Signal Processing with Emphasis on Underwater Accoustics*. Reprinted in Childers (1978), pp. 42-48.

Burg, J. P.: 1975, *Maximum Entropy Spectral Analysis*, PhD thesis, Stanford University.

Burns, A. F. and Mitchell, W. C.: 1946, *Measuring Business Cycles*, National Bureau of Economic Research, New York.

Cargill, T. F.: 1974, Early applications of spectral methods to economic time series, *History of Political Economy* 6, 1–16.

Chadha, B. and Prasad, E.: 1994, Are prices countercyclical? evidence from the G-7, IMF Working Paper WP/94/91.

Chan, K. H., Hayya, J. C. and Ord, J. K.: 1977, A note on trend removal methods: The case of polynomial regression versus variate differencing, *Econometrica* 45, 737–744.

Childers, D. G.: 1978, *Modern Spectrum Analysis*, IEEE Press, New York.

Correia, I., Neves, J. L. and Rebelo, S.: 1992, Business cylces from 1850 to 1950: New facts about old data, *European Economic Review* 36, 459–467.

Crum, W. L.: 1923, Cycles of rates on commercial paper, *The Review of Economics and Statistics* 5, 17–27.

Darnell, A. C. and Evans, J. L.: 1990, *The Limits of Econometrics*, Edward Elgar, Aldershot.

Davis, H. T.: 1941, *The Analysis of Economic Time Series*, Principia Press, San Antonio, Texas. (Reprinted 1963).

Dickey, D. A.: 1976, *Estimation and Hypothesis Testing in Nonstationary Time Series*, PhD thesis, Iowa State University.

Dickey, D. A. and Fuller, W. A.: 1979, Distribution of the estimators for autoregressive time series with a unit root, *Journal of the American Statistical Association* 74, 427–431.

Dickey, D. A. and Fuller, W. A.: 1981, Likelihood ratio statistics for autoregressive time series with a unit root, *Econometrica* 49, 1057–1072.

Dickey, D. A., Bell, W. R. and Miller, R. B.: 1986, Unit roots in time series models: Tests and implications, *American Statistician* **40**, 12–26.

Englund, P., Persson, T. and Svensson, L. E. O.: 1992, Swedish business cycles, 1861-1988, *Journal of Monetary Economics* **30**, 343–371.

Fiorito, R. and Kollintzas, T.: 1992, Stylized facts of business cycles in the G7 from a real business cycles perspective, Center for Economic Policy Research, Discussion Paper No. 681.

Fougere, P. F.: 1985, A review of the problem of spontaneous line splitting in Maximum Entropy power spectral analysis, *in* C. R. Smith and W. Grandy (eds), *Maximum–Entropy and Bayesian Methods in Inverse Problems*, D. Reidel Publishing Company, Dordrecht, pp. 303–314.

Frisch, R.: 1933a, Editorial, *Econometrica* **1**, 1–4.

Frisch, R.: 1933b, Propagation problems and impulse problems in dynamic economics, *Economic Essays in Honor of Gustav Cassel*, George Allen & Unwin, London. Reprinted in Gordon and Klein (1965).

Fuller, W. A.: 1976, *Introduction to Statistical Time Series*, John Wiley & Sons, New York, Chichester, Brisbane, Toronto, Singapore.

Geyer, A.: 1985, *Maximum–Entropie–Spektralanalyse ökonomischer Zeitreihen*, VWGÖ, Wien.

Gordon, R. A. and Klein, L. R.: 1965, *Readings in Business Cycles*, Richard D. Irwin, Homewood, Ill.

Granger, C. W. J.: 1966, The typical spectral shape of an economic variable, *Econometrica* **34**, 151–161.

Granger, C. W. J. and Engle, R. F.: 1983, Applications of spectral analysis in econometrics, *in* D. Brillinger and P. Krishnaia (eds), *Handbook of Statistics, Vol. 3*, Elsevier Science Publishers B.V., Amsterdam.

Granger, C. W. J. and Newbold, P.: 1986, *Forecasting Economic Time Series*, 2nd edn, Academic Press, London.

Greene, W. H.: 1993, *Econometric Analysis*, 2nd edn, Macmillan, New York, Toronto, Oxford, Singapore.

Greenstein, B.: 1935, Periodogram analysis with special application to business failures in the United States, 1867-1932, *Econometrica* **3**, 170–198.

Grenander, U.: 1958, Bandwidth and variance of the spectrum, *Journal of the Royal Statistical Society, Series B* **20**, 152–157.

Hamilton, J. D.: 1989, A new approach to the economic analysis of nonstationary time series and the business cycle, *Econometrica* **57**, 357–384.

Härdle, W.: 1991, *Smoothing Techniques with Implementation in S*, Springer, New York.

Harvey, A. C.: 1992, *Forecasting, Structural Time Series Models and the Kalman Filter*, Cambridge University Press, Cambridge.

Harvey, A. C.: 1993, *Time Series Models*, 2nd edn, Harvester Wheatsheaf, New York, London, Toronto, Sydney, Tokio, Singapore.

Harvey, A. C. and Collier, G.: 1977, Testing for functional misspecification in regression analysis, *Journal of Econometrics* **6**, 103–119.

Harvey, A. C. and Jaeger, A.: 1991, Detrending, stylized facts and the business cycle, London School of Economics, Discussion Paper No.EM/91/230.

Heintel, M.: 1994, A bayesian way to identify the order of autoregressive processes, Münchner Wirtschaftswissenschaftliche Beiträge.

Helmstädter, E.: 1989, Die M-Form des Wachstumszyklus, *Jahrbücher für Nationalökonomie und Statistik* **206**, 383–394.

Hicks, J.: 1950, *A Contribution to the Theory of the Trade Cycle*, Clarendon Press, Oxford.

Hicks, J.: 1965, *Capital and Growth*, Oxford University Press, London.

Hillinger, C.: 1992a, The methodology of empirical science, *in* C. Hillinger (ed.), *Cyclical Growth in Market and Planned Economies*, Oxford University Press, London, pp. 47–60.

Hillinger, C.: 1992b, Paradigm change and scientific method in the study of economic fluctuations, *in* C. Hillinger (ed.), *Cyclical Growth in Market and Planned Economies*, Oxford University Press, London, pp. 5–46.

Hillinger, C. and Reiter, M.: 1992, The quantitative and qualitative explanation of macroeconomic investment and production cycles, *in* C. Hillinger (ed.), *Cyclical Growth in Market and Planned Economies*, Oxford University Press, Oxford, pp. 111–140.

Hillinger, C. and Sebold-Bender, M.: 1992, The stylized facts of macroeconomic fluctuations, *in* C. Hillinger (ed.), *Cyclical Growth in Market and Planned Economies*, Oxford University Press, London, pp. 63–110.

Hillinger, C., Reiter, M. and Weser, T.: 1992a, Micro foundations of the second-order accelerator and of cyclical behaviour, *in* C. Hillinger (ed.), *Cyclical Growth in Market and Planned Economies*, Oxford University Press, Oxford, pp. 167–180.

Hillinger, C., Reiter, M. and Woitek, U.: 1992b, Model–independent detrending for determining the cyclical properties of macroeconomic time series, Münchner Wirtschaftswissenschaftliche Beiträge.

Hodrick, R. and Prescott, E.: 1980, Postwar U.S. business cycles: An empirical investigation, Discussion Paper No. 451, Carnegie-Mellon University.

Hylleberg, S.: 1992, *Modelling Seasonality*, Oxford University Press, Oxford.

Jaynes, E.: 1985, Where do we go from here?, *in* C. R. Smith and W. Grandy (eds), *Maximum-Entropy and Bayesian Methods in Inverse Problems*, D. Reidel Publishing Company, Dordrecht, pp. 21–58.

Juglar, C.: 1889, *Des Crises Commerciales et de leur Retour Periodique en France, en Angleterre et aux États-Unis*, 2 edn, Guillaumin, Paris.

Kay, S. M.: 1988, *Modern Spectral Estimation: Theory and Application*, Prentice Hall, Englewood Cliffs.

King, R. G. and Rebelo, S. T.: 1993, Low frequency filtering and real business cycles, *Journal of Economic Dynamics and Control* **17**, 207–231.

Kitchin, J.: 1923, Cycles and trends in economic factors, *Review of Economics and Statistics* **5**, 10–17.

Koopmans, L. H.: 1974, *The Spectral Analysis of Time Series*, Academic Press, New York, San Francisco, London.

Koopmans, L. H.: 1983, A spectral analysis primer, *in* D. Brilliger and P. Krishnaia (eds), *Handbook of Statistics*, Elsevier Science Publishers B.V.

Koopmans, T. C.: 1947, Measurement without theory, *Review of Economic Statistics* **29**, 161–172. Reprinted in Gordon and Klein (1965), pp. 186-203.

Kuznets, S.: 1958, Long swings in the growth of population and in related economic variables, *Proceedings of the American Philosphical Society* **102**, 25–57.

Kwiatkowsky, D., Phillips, P. C. and Schmidt, P.: 1991, Testing the null hypothesis of stationarity against the alternative of a unit root: How sure are we that economic time series have a unit root?, Cowles Foundation Discussion Paper No. 979.

Kydland, F. E. and Prescott, E. C.: 1990, Business cycles: Real facts and a monetary myth, *Federal Reserve Bank of Minneapolis, Quarterly Review* **14**, 3–18.

Ljung, G. M. and Box, G. E. P.: 1978, On a measure of lack of fit in time series models, *Biometrika* **66**, 67–72.

Lucas, R. E.: 1977, Understanding business cycles, *in* K. Brunner and A. Metzler (eds), *Stabilization of the Domestic and International Economy, Carnegie-Rochester Series on Public Policy, Vol.5.* Reprinted in Lucas (1981), pp. 215-239.

Lucas, R. E.: 1981, *Studies in Business-Cycle Theory*, Basil Blackwell, Oxford.

Lütkepohl, H.: 1991, *Introduction to Multiple Time Series Analysis*, Springer, Berlin, Heidelberg, New York, Tokio.

Marple, S. L.: 1987, *Digital Spectral Analysis with Applications*, Prentice Hall, Englewood Cliffs.

Maußner, A.: 1994, *Konjunkturtheorie*, Springer, Berlin, Heidelberg, New York, Tokyo.

Mitchell, W. C.: 1927, *Business Cycles: The Problem and Its Setting*, National Bureau of Economic Research, New York. (13th Reprint, 1946).

Moore, G. H. and Zarnowitz, V.: 1986, The development and role of the National Bureau of Economic Research's business cycle chronologies, *in* R. J. Gordon (ed.), *The American Business Cycle. Continuity and Change*, University of Chicago Press, Chicago, London, pp. 735–779.

Moore, H. L.: 1914, *Economic Cycles - Their Law and Their Cause*, Macmillan, New York.

Moore, H. L.: 1923, *Generating Economic Cycles*, Macmillan, New York.

Morf, M., Vieira, A., Lee, D. T. and Kailath, T.: 1978, Recursive multichannel maximum entropy spectral estimation, *IEEE Transactions on Geoscience Electronics*.

Morgan, M. S.: 1990, *The History of Econometric Ideas*, Cambridge University Press, Cambridge.

Nelson, C. R. and Plosser, C. I.: 1982, Trends and random walks in macroeconomic time series, *Journal of Monetary Economics* **10**, 139–162.

Niehans, J.: 1992, Juglar's credit cycles, *History of Political Economy* **24**, 545–569.

Parzen, E.: 1974, Some recent advances in time series analysis, *IEEE Transactions on Automatic Control* **AC-19**, 723–729.

Perron, P.: 1988, Trends and random walks in macroeconomic time series: Further evidence from a new approach, *Journal of Economic Dynamics and Control* **12**, 297–332.

Perron, P.: 1989, The great crash, the oil price shock, and the unit root hypothesis, *Econometrica* **57**, 1361–1402.

Phillips, P. C.: 1987, Time series regression with a unit root, *Econometrica* **55**, 277–301.

Phillips, P. C. and Perron, P.: 1988, Testing for a unit root in time series regression, *Biometrika* **75**, 599–607.

Priestley, M.: 1981, *Spectral Analysis and Time Series*, Academic Press, London.

Reiter, M.: 1995, *The Dynamics of Business Cycles*, Physica, Heidelberg, New York.

Romer, C. D.: 1986, Is the stabilization of the postwar economy a figment of the data?, *American Economic Review* **76**, 314–334.

Romer, C. D.: 1989, The prewar business cycle reconsidered: New estimates of GNP, 1869-1908, *Journal of Political Economy* **97**, 1–37.

Rudebusch, G. D.: 1992, Trends and random walks in macroeconomic time series: A re-examination, *International Economic Review* **33**, 616–680.

Rudebusch, G. D.: 1993, The uncertain unit root in real GDP, *American Economic Review* **83**, 264–272.

Samuelson, P. A.: 1961, *Economics. An Introductory Analysis*, 5 edn, McGraw-Hill, New York, Toronto, London.

Sargent, T. J.: 1979, *Macroeconomic Theory*, Academic Press, New York, San Francisco, London.

Schebeck, F. and Tichy, G.: 1984, Die "Stylized Facts" in der modernen Konjunkturdiskussion, *in* G. Bombach, B. Gahlen and A. E. Ott (eds), *Perspektiven der Konjunkturforschung*, J. C. B. Mohr, Tübingen, pp. 207–224.

Schuster, A.: 1898, On the investigation of hidden periodicities with application to a supposed twenty-six-day period of meteorological phenomena, *Terrestrial Magnetism* **3**, 13–41.

Sebold-Bender, M.: 1990, *Stilisierte Fakten makroökonomischer Schwankungen*, PhD thesis, University of Munich.

Sebold-Bender, M.: 1992, Inventories in macroeconomic fluctuations: The stylized facts, *International Journal of Production Economics* **26**, 107–114.

Sims, C. A.: 1980, Macroeconomics and reality, *Econometrica* **48**, 1–48.

Smeets, H.-D.: 1992, "Stylized Facts"zum Konjunkturverlauf der Bundesrepublik Deutschland, *Jahrbücher für Nationalökonomie und Statistik* **210**, 512–532.

Summers, L. H.: 1991, The scientific illusion in empirical macroeconomics, *Scandinavian Journal of Economics* **93**, 129–148.

Swingler, D.: 1979, A comparison between Burg's Maximum Entropy method and a nonrecursive technique for the spectral analysis of deterministic signals, *Journal of Geophysical Research* **84**, 679–685.

Tichy, G.: 1994, *Konjunktur. Stilisierte Fakten, Theorie, Prognose.*, 2 edn, Springer, Berlin, Heidelberg, New York, Tokyo.

Urquhart, M.: 1986, New estimates of GNP, Canada, 1870-1926: Some implications for Canadian development, *in* S. Engerman and R. Gallman (eds), *Long-Term Factors in American Economic Growth*, University of Chicago Press, Chicago, pp. 9–94.

Weser, T.: 1992, The aggregation problem for economic cycles, *in* C. Hillinger (ed.), *Cyclical Growth in Market and Planned Economies*, Oxford University Press, Oxford, pp. 181–200.

West, K. D.: 1988, On the interpretation of near random-walk behaviour in GNP, *American Economic Review* **78**, 202–209.

Wilson, E. B.: 1934, The periodogram of American business activity, *Quarterly Journal of Economics* **48**, 375–417.

Woitek, U.: 1996, The G7-countries: A multivariate description of business cycle stylized facts, *in* W. Barnett, G. Gandolfo and C. Hillinger (eds), *Dynamic Disequilibrium Modelling: Theory and Applications*, Cambridge University Press, Cambridge, chapter 10, pp. 283–309.

Zarnowitz, V.: 1985, Recent work on business cycles in historical perspective: A review of theories and evidence, *Journal of Economic Literature* **XXIII**, 523–580.

Zarnowitz, V.: 1992, *Business Cycles. Theory, History, Indicators, and Forecasting*, University of Chicago Press, Chicago, London.

Index

Druck: STRAUSS OFFSETDRUCK, MÖRLENBACH
Verarbeitung: SCHÄFFER, GRÜNSTADT